Fighter

Fighter

The Unauthorized Biography of
Georges St-Pierre

JERRY LANGTON

John Wiley & Sons Canada, Ltd.

Library and Archives Canada Cataloguing in Publication

Langton, Jerry, 1965–
    Fighter : the unauthorized biography of Georges St-Pierre, UFC champion / Jerry Langton.

Includes index.
Issued also in electronic formats.
ISBN 978-1-118008-03-4

    1. St-Pierre, Georges, 1981–. 2. Martial artists—Canada—Biography. I. Title.

GV1113.S23L35 2011   796.8092   C2010-906803-3

ISBN 978-1-118008-03-4 (print); 978-1-118-01734-0 (eMobi); 978-1-118-01739-5 (ePub) 978-1-118-017388 (ePDF)

Production Credits
Cover design: Kerrin Hands
Cover Photo Credit: Josh Hedges/Zuffa LLC/Getty Images Sport/Getty Images
Interior design: Adrian So
Typesetter: Natalia Burobina
Printer: Friesens Printing Ltd.

Editorial Credits
Executive Editor: Don Loney
Production Editor: Pauline Ricablanca
Editorial Assistant: Brian Will

John Wiley & Sons Canada, Ltd.
6045 Freemont Blvd.
Mississauga, Ontario
L5R 4J3

Printed in Canada

1 2 3 4 5 FP 15 14 13 12 11

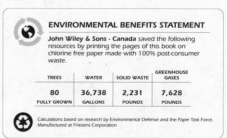

ENVIRONMENTAL BENEFITS STATEMENT

John Wiley & Sons - Canada saved the following resources by printing the pages of this book on chlorine free paper made with 100% post-consumer waste.

TREES	WATER	SOLID WASTE	GREENHOUSE GASES
80	36,738	2,231	7,628
FULLY GROWN	GALLONS	POUNDS	POUNDS

Calculations based on research by Environmental Defense and the Paper Task Force. Manufactured at Friesens Corporation

INTRODUCTION

It was a huge event, even by UFC standards. There were thousands of people in the massive Prudential Center in Newark, New Jersey, and millions around the world watching *UFC 111: St-Pierre vs. Hardy* on March 27, 2010. Their attention was focused on a four-foot-high platform. On it was an almost-32-foot-wide octagonal cage made up of a chain-link fence covered in black vinyl. Inside were three men: the referee, Georges St-Pierre, and the man he was about to fight, Dan "The Outlaw" Hardy. It was a much-anticipated welterweight championship bout, part of the increasingly popular Ultimate Fighting Championship (UFC).

St-Pierre, at 5-foot-10 and a fighting weight of 170 pounds, is not a large man. But he is incredibly popular. Rogers Sportsnet, an ESPN-like Canadian media conglomerate, had just named him "Canadian Athlete of the Year" for three years running—2008, 2009 and 2010. St-Pierre—better known by his nicknames "Rush" and "GSP"—is the second-most-popular and -bankable athlete in Canada, behind only hockey superstar Sidney Crosby, and ranks well ahead of such luminaries as two-time NBA MVP Steve Nash and Major League Baseball stars Justin Morneau and Jason Bay. You can even buy a GSP action figure.

But he's more than just a Canadian phenomenon. *Sports Illustrated* declared him "Fighter of the Year," and Spike TV, the U.S.-based cable network aimed at men, gave him their coveted "Most Dangerous Man" award. He's broken through the big barrier, the one that separates mainstream sports from niche sports. While many other UFC fighters are sponsored by gyms and mixed martial arts gear suppliers, GSP has endorsement deals from huge corporations. He represents international brands Gatorade and Under Armour. (Gatorade is owned by PepsiCo, and Under Armour is also represented by people like Olympic swimmer Michael Phelps, star linebacker Ray Lewis and wrestler-turned-movie-star Dwayne Johnson.) They don't sponsor the UFC or any other fighter, just him. In his own quiet way, GSP has brought enough legitimacy to mixed martial arts fighting that even the corporate big guys want him in their tent.

As tradition dictates, Hardy, the challenger, entered the Octagon first. His entrance music was "England Belongs to Me" by Cock Sparrer. One of the original punk rock bands from the 1970s—there's a story that impresario Malcolm McLaren wanted to sign them in 1976 to perform alongside the Sex Pistols, but the band's members refused because he wouldn't buy them beer— Cock Sparrer was relegated to "where-are-they-now?" status until Hardy helped repopularize them. The version of "England Belongs to Me" they play when he enters the ring isn't the band's original 1982 recording, but a new one called "The Dan Hardy Version" on which he actually sings.

Tall and sinewy, Hardy looks like a fighter or perhaps a football wide receiver. He has a large tattoo on his belly. It's a Buddhist mantra written in Sanskrit. The tattoo reads "Om mani padme hum." It has no literal meaning in English, but is a short prayer intended to protect the chanter and to remind him of a number of important truths, including charity and humility. Although it is not an overtly political message, the UFC decided to digitally remove it from Hardy's belly in all promotional materials, probably because it is frequently associated with the Dalai Lama, a harsh opponent of China's continuing occupation of his native Tibet.

When asked why, UFC president Dana White said it was an economic decision, based on his desire to export his product to China's 1.3 billion people. "I'm trying to get into China," he said matter-of-factly. "I don't need anti-Chinese government stuff on my fighters."

When Hardy found out that his tattoo had been revised by the league, he was surprised because he didn't consider it a political statement, but a personal one. "It's basically just like a prayer for focus," he told reporters. "It keeps me walking the path that I should be walking without veering off and distracting myself."

Aside from the tattoo, what stood out about Hardy were his strong-looking body, his fighter's face and his bright-red Mohawk.

Then everything changed. As soon as the opening strains of Notorious B.I.G.'s "Juicy" could be heard, the crowd ignited. It's an interesting choice for an introductory song. It's a semi-autobiographical allegory in which B.I.G.—a former crack dealer turned millionaire rapper—sneers at everybody who doubted his rise to fame would happen.

Shorter and stouter than Hardy, GSP has a very distinctive shape. He has very broad shoulders and long, thick arms. His legs are solidly muscular, but he has a surprisingly thin waist and his hips look almost tiny for a man his size. His head is shaved almost to the skin, and he has two small and tasteful tattoos—the word for jiu-jitsu written in kanji (Chinese characters) on the right side of his chest and a large fleur-de-lis on his right calf. His confidence showed immediately. GSP quickly took control of the center of the Octagon, forcing Hardy to circle him, sizing him up for weaknesses while staying out of the reach of his lightning-quick hands and feet. Twenty-five seconds into the bout, GSP shocked Hardy with a quick charge and took him to the ground in one fleet motion.

The crowd in New Jersey was delighted to see GSP take Hardy down. But he wasn't completely in charge. Hardy wrapped his legs around GSP in a move jiu-jitsu practitioners call "taking guard." Using his natural cunning, strength and an amazing amount of grit, Hardy managed to get to his knees and, later, his feet. The first round continued like that—Hardy avoiding, GSP attacking.

The second round started, and GSP again took the center immediately. The fighters exchanged jabs. Nobody really connected. Then, in a flash, Hardy was on the ground. Throughout the rest of the round, GSP punished Hardy in a variety of ways, but failed to put him away.

The third round was a lot like the first. GSP quickly took the center, Hardy whipped out a hard right. It was a big mistake, and GSP made him pay for it, bringing him to the ground quickly. Hardy stayed tough, maintaining guard, but GSP began hammering the challenger's face with his elbow. Hardy, pawing at his own eye, was clearly on the defensive. Hardy took a chance. He reached up, hoping to trap GSP's head between his legs for a triangle choke. But GSP, clearly predicting such a move, slid the challenger around and grabbed his left arm. He was just about to twist it and secure the fight. This move—called a "kimura" after the great Japanese judo master Masahiko Kimura—is one of the most basic and effective ways to secure a submission. But Hardy worked his way free and got to his feet. GSP pulled him back down again. Even the most neophyte UFC viewer could tell Hardy was in trouble.

He was turning red and breathing hard. He worked desperately to get back on his knees, but GSP was hammering him from above the whole time. Miraculously, he got to his feet, but GSP quickly locked his legs and brought him to the ground again. The round ended there. Hardy was once again saved by the bell.

Round Four started with Hardy woozy, but aggressive. A few seconds in, Hardy actually landed a jab to GSP's cheek. After absorbing the blow, GSP deftly took advantage of Hardy's momentary loss of balance, grabbed his arm and brought him back down to the ground. Before he even hit the mat, Hardy took two nasty shots from GSP's right hand. GSP got his left arm in a kimura. You could see the pain on Hardy's face. He slipped out, but was no sooner on his feet than GSP brought him down again. With Hardy basically at his mercy, GSP showed kimura again, but surprised the crowd by applying a knee bar instead. Hardy was in unbelievable agony when the round mercifully ended.

The fifth round began with GSP landing a short jab. The fighters exchanged kicks, then GSP struck with the quickness of a rattlesnake. Hardy was on the ground yet again. He attempted to get GSP's head under his leg to apply a triangle choke, but GSP shook it off easily. GSP deftly pressed down on Hardy's chest with his own, keeping him immobile. GSP drove his knees into Hardy's ribs. Hardy coughed and rolled away. GSP was back on him immediately, again using his chest as a weapon to keep Hardy down. He was patient, attempting all kinds of moves in rapid succession to try to find his opponent's weakest spot. Hardy was valiantly fighting off these forays, but they left him so busy that he couldn't mount any attacks of his own or even try to escape from underneath the champ.

GSP decided to work Hardy's left arm. He had just about got him into an arm triangle hold when Hardy rolled out of his grasp.

Somehow, he managed to get to his knees and then, eventually, excruciatingly, to his feet. But the champ would have none of it and unceremoniously dumped Hardy to the mat again. GSP got him into a leg lock, and you could see that Hardy was in extreme pain, but time ran out without a knockout or a submission.

GSP had successfully defended his welterweight title. He showed why he was champion and he made some new fans. The crowd seemed happy—their champ had come through again. Hardy had fought valiantly, but was dominated by GSP. The Internet was alive with praise for the man. Much of the online conversation centered on one topic: since there is nobody close to his own weight who had even the slightest hope of beating him, should GSP add weight to move up a class?

But he also gave his detractors fuel to criticize him. Sure he had dominated Hardy, but he hadn't *destroyed* him. There are lots of people out there for whom the win is secondary to the show. They aren't out for blood exactly, but they want to see two men go into the ring and only one come out with his head held high. They want a knockout or a tapout, not another decision, no matter how heavily in favor of the champ it was.

Even Hardy got into the act. "I was saying this in the buildup to the fight—GSP doesn't take risks in his fights anymore," he said. "He knew that my strength was striking and 17 seconds [into] the first round, he shot in for a takedown. I think that says a lot about his approach to the fight game. He goes in there to win the fight and keep the belt and not to beat his opponent. You can only fight this way for so long before people start complaining."

And the league itself appeared to agree with that line of thinking. After the fight, a reporter collared Dana White for an interview, pointing out that there was a great deal of criticism of

GSP's performance against Hardy, particularly in the British media, which had likened him to Floyd Mayweather Jr.—a welterweight champion boxer with a 41–0 record and a reputation as being a methodical, defense-minded fighter who is effective but tedious to watch. White responded, surprisingly, by siding with the critics over his champion. "Listen, every fight you have is not going to be the most exciting fight in the world, and you know me—I want exciting fights," he said. "But Georges St-Pierre, he went out there, it was a dominant performance." Then he shrugged and added. "He's unhappy with his performance too . . . he wanted to do better, I obviously wanted better, but Dan Hardy came to fight."

When asked if the "boring" fight would hurt GSP's reputation or future UFC pay-per-view sales, White responded:

> I don't think so. He's the best 170-pounder in the world, one of the best pound-for-pound fighters in the world. And I think people love him, man. Listen, the kid sits up here and he's so classy and he sits there and admits he wishes he did better. And, you know, people just love him. And not every fight you have is going to be the best fight you've ever done, but I think because of this fight he's going to come out and look better next time.

At the press conference itself, White (in a sports jacket and black shirt) held the dais while GSP sat next to him. In front of him were a few drinks and his UFC Championship belt with a buckle as big as a pizza. He wore a very tasteful chalk-striped navy suit with a white shirt and a light blue silk tie. Aside from some bruising on his face, he could have been a corporate talking head announcing a recall or a film director promoting his latest project. He looked a little tense, but very composed. He spoke from where he sat. In accented but well-spoken English, he said:

I'm going to tell you the truth, I'm not happy about my performance. I won the fight, but it's like—to make a similarity—it's like a sprinter, a 100-meter sprinter, who is world champion. He sprints and wins the 100-meter in, let's say, 10 seconds. And a few months later, he has another race. He wins again, but he wins in 10 seconds again, still. So, he won't be happy. He still is world champion, but he hasn't beaten his time. It's a little bit [like] the same thing that happened to me tonight. I won, but I haven't beaten my performance of last time. So I'm not happy. I wanted to finish. You know, have a clean win and, for me, like this, it's not clean.

I tried too much to go for the submission. Instead, I should have . . . you know, in boxing they have a saying: "If you go for the knockout, the knockout doesn't come." The same thing can happen in mixed martial arts; if you go too much for the submission, the submission doesn't come. You have to let the opportunity come. And tonight I tried to . . . sometimes I had the position, I tried to use to my [advantage] because I've gained a lot. I'm a lot more powerful and I'm . . . bigger than I was. So I try sometimes to power out some arm bars, some kimuras, and I forgot the technical element of it. And sometimes those little details make the difference. Like the angle, the leverage, the way you're positioning—that's what makes the finish. And tonight, when I had the kimura, I made a mistake, a technical mistake . . . the arm bar was not as it should be. Next time, that won't happen. Now I know what I did wrong.

He then described in minute detail how Hardy was able to escape his kimura and how he had learned from his mistakes. It was an almost scientific examination of Hardy's use of leverage and his own misunderstanding of angles and underestimation of Hardy's breaking point combined to prevent the kimura.

White then retook center stage and said his "Twitter was blowing up" with fan complaints about the main event. He seemed particularly insulted by one tweet that compared the fight to college wrestling.

After that, GSP held a Q&A session with reporters. He said all the right things about respecting other fighters, hoping to be a champion for a long, long time and wanting his fights to be exciting enough to bring more fans to the UFC. It may be the most timeworn of sporting clichés, but in this case it's true. Being the best in the world simply isn't good enough for GSP.

CHAPTER

Historians differ as to the exact origin of Asian martial arts, but most tie its beginnings to India, where Buddhism, yoga and nata dancing all contain elements that would later become vital parts of most martial arts styles. Interestingly, at least some scholars believe the catalyst that turned those other pursuits into fighting sports was none other than *pankration*, introduced by Alexander the Great of Macedon, a Greek emperor whose realm, at its peak, extended all the way to India.

However it started, the earliest recorded reference to martial arts came in the fifth century when the Chinese government caught Buddhist monks storing arms and learning how to fight. The preeminent monastery among these was the Shaolin Temple in Northeastern China, which was founded in 464.

Then, a Buddhist monk appeared from the West and changed the Eastern world profoundly. Little biographical knowledge can be gleaned about Bodhidharma from contemporary records, but there is general agreement as to who he was, where he came from and what he did. Bodhidharma was probably born into a warrior caste somewhere in India, perhaps just before the beginning of the sixth century. He became a Buddhist monk and traveled eastward in search of enlightenment. He was a big man, and is traditionally portrayed as having a long beard, heavy eyebrows and a hairy chest and arms. Many accounts refer to him as a "blue-eyed barbarian from the West," so he may have been from even farther away than India. He was impatient and known to be quick to anger.

But he had an idea. His philosophies—later collectively known as Zen—became immensely popular and his reputation grew from respected to revered. When he arrived at the Shaolin Temple, he was said to have been disgusted with the physical shape the monks were in. Wong Kiew Kit, a contemporary Shaolin monk and kung fu master, describes Bodhidharma's immediate influence:

> It was during this time that the venerable Bodhidharma came from India to China to spread Buddhism. In 527 he settled down in the Shaolin monastery in Henan province and inspired the development of Shaolin Kung Fu. This marked a watershed in the history of Kung Fu, because it led to a change of course, as kung fu became institutionalized. Before this, martial arts were known only in general sense.

The Shaolin Monastery has been the center of kung fu learning ever since. As Buddhism, Zen and other concepts spread through eastern Asia, they took the practices of kung fu with them and they developed into hundreds of diverse types of martial arts, from taekwondo to sumo.

Invasion and colonization of much of eastern Asia by European powers in the nineteenth century brought an immense number of firearms into the region, and the need for hand-to-hand combat

(and with it, unarmed martial arts) began to wane. It was still prac-
ticed as a sport and an art, but in many places it seemed arcane.

Beginning in about 1890, European interest in Asian martial arts brought a small stream of practitioners to the West, but
their skills were generally seen as exhibitions of exotic Eastern
traditions, not as sport. Many of these styles of combat involved
kicking, which Westerners considered an unmanly, even devious,
way to fight.

Four profound events of the middle of the twentieth century—the end of the Second World War in 1945, the Communist
takeover of mainland China in 1949, the end of open hostilities
in the Korean conflict in 1953 and the end of U.S. involvement
in the Southeast Asian conflict in 1973—changed things. Previous
Asian immigration to the West had been small-scale, and those
who did arrive stayed in tightly knit communities. But now there
were waves of Japanese, Chinese, Taiwanese, Korean, Vietnamese,
Cambodian, Laotian and Thai arrivals, and they brought many diverse types of martial arts with them.

Japanese styles were the first to come into Western conscious-
ness. Karate—originally from the Ryukyu Islands—is a striking
style that depends on both punching and kicking. It became well
known and later, when it was successfully marketed as a way for
smaller boys and men to fight back against much larger bullies,
it became well used. Judo became popular in the media if not in
practice, although most Westerners knew it from the concept of a
strike called the "judo chop," even though judo is predominantly a
grappling style of fighting.

Asian martial arts could well have faded from Western consciousness had there not been a true champion for it. In the
early morning of November 27, 1940, Lee Hoi-chuen—a singer
from Hong Kong who was on tour in the United States with the

Cantonese Opera Company—rushed his German-Chinese wife, Grace Ho, to Jackson Street Hospital in San Francisco's Chinatown. In the year and hour of the Dragon, she gave birth to a healthy baby boy.

Ho, who had fallen in love with America and hoped to come back some day, named the boy Lee Jun-fan, which means "return again in prosperity" in Cantonese. A maternity-ward nurse grew attached to the bright-faced boy but couldn't pronounce his given name, so she started calling him Bruce.

Following Lee's tour, the family returned to China. After being kicked out of a series of high schools for low marks and fighting, Bruce ended up in a Catholic high school where he was mentored in Western-style boxing. He was extremely well suited to the sport and won two high school boxing championships. In fact, only one opponent ever made it out of the first round against him, and he only managed to survive until the third.

Lee was a good fighter, very good. He had an uncanny ability to think and react quickly and to mix styles as the fight progressed. He quickly became the leader of a gang of street toughs that called themselves "The Tigers of Junction Street," although he lived around the corner on Nathan Street (the site of his house is now covered by a shopping mall). And he ran into trouble. The police told his family that if they caught him fighting one more time, he'd go to jail. And some friends told them that Lee had beaten up the wrong man, a member of the local triad, and that the gang had put a price on his head.

That was enough for his parents, who sent Lee (now widely known as Bruce) to join his older sister Agnes, who was living with friends in San Francisco. With $100 in his pocket, which he earned on the journey by giving cha-cha lessons to first-class passengers, he instead moved to Seattle, where he lived with and worked for family friend Ruby Chow. A remarkable woman, Chow opened the first Chinese restaurant in Seattle outside Chinatown and served three terms on county council. And she was strict with Lee, offering him room in the restaurant's attic and board in exchange for hours of hard work, graduating high school and college and keeping his fights inside the ring. He also made extra money giving dance lessons.

Lee graduated high school and attended Edison Technical School (now called Seattle Central Community College) before moving up to the University of Washington. Lee told his family and friends he was studying philosophy, but was actually enrolled in the school's dramatic arts program. He financed his tuition and lifestyle by providing martial arts lessons, eventually opening Lee Jun Fan Gung Fu Institute (he preferred to use the Cantonese "gung fu" over the more universally accepted Mandarin "kung fu"). The school proved successful, and Lee dropped out of college in 1964. He and a friend, James Yimm Lee, relocated the school to Oakland, California. There, they made a valuable connection—Ed Parker. Parker was a rare American martial arts master—he developed his own style called American kenpo, which was a very fast-moving style of karate. Lee not only learned kenpo from him but he also received an invitation to perform at the Long Beach International Karate Championship in 1964.

Bruce made yet another connection. His new friend, Jhoon Goo Rhee, was a Korean taekwondo master who, like Lee, had put up with a great deal of criticism for teaching martial arts to non-Asians. In exchange for some of Lee's best moves, Rhee taught Lee some of the most effective taekwondo kicks.

At about that time, Lee came to an epiphany. He realized that his combination of wing chun, tai chi chuan, boxing, American kenpo and taekwondo was far more effective than using any one discipline. He knew that he was the best fighter in the world not because he was the master of a martial art, but because he had managed to mix the best of many of them while disregarding the parts he did not need. And, still angered by martial arts masters who refused to teach non-pureblood Asian students, he was determined to teach anyone who wanted to learn. With that new philosophy, Lee established his own fighting style that sacrificed the stodgy formalities of traditional martial arts and substituted them with moves he knew from experience would win fights. He called this new style jeet kune do (which means "the way of the intercepting fist").

But in 1970, Lee suffered a debilitating injury. While performing a "good morning" exercise—in which he placed a barbell that weighed almost as much as he did on his shoulders and bent down from the waist, he injured a nerve in his pelvis. Doctors ordered an indefinite term of bed rest and told him he'd never perform martial arts again. Lee did take some time off—in fact, he used it to develop the TV series that later became *Kung Fu*, which he planned to star in—and eventually regained his strength.

Despite earlier success in appearing in *The Green Hornet* and *Batman*, after the injury Hollywood wanted nothing to do with him, so he went back to Hong Kong. He starred in three local films—later known in the West as *Fists of Fury*, *The Chinese Connection* and *The Way of the Dragon*. They were simple local-kid-gets-bullied-then-takes-his-revenge stories, but they were just what Hong Kong's audiences wanted and they were huge blockbusters by regional standards.

Hollywood couldn't ignore him anymore and he returned to film *Enter the Dragon* in 1973. It's a silly plot, many of the performances are poor and the production values vary considerably. But

Lee was masterful in it and captured the imaginations of Western audiences just as he had those in Hong Kong. For an $850,000 investment, producers would realize more than $25 million in gross earnings, and the film achieved a cult status that survives today.

But Lee wouldn't live to see it. A number of his fellow cast members noticed that Lee wasn't feeling well during the dubbing and looping of the film's soundtrack. He collapsed at a dubbing session on May 10, 1973, and was rushed to Hong Kong Baptist Hospital. His diagnosis was not promising; Lee had a cerebral edema, an in-cranium swelling commonly known as "water on the brain." Doctors reduced the swelling and prescribed a diuretic. On June 20, 1973, Lee was meeting with producer Raymond Chow and actress Betty Ting Pei at her Hong Kong apartment when he complained of a headache. Chow left for a dinner meeting, and Lee retired to the couch for a nap. Pei offered him a pill she took by prescription, an aspirin-based painkiller called Equagesic that is no longer legal in many countries. Lee took one and never woke up from his nap. When Pei could not wake him, she called an ambulance. Doctors at Queen Elizabeth Hospital said that he had an allergic reaction to the Equagesic, which worsened his edema, and that he died "via misadventure."

Despite his short career and limited exposure to Western audiences, Lee is probably the most famous and successful fighter of all time. Of course, his good looks and winning personality had a lot to do with it, but the fact that such a small man could not just beat, but literally destroy far bigger opponents was a big part of what put him on top. And the way he did it—by taking the best of various martial arts and putting them together as the fight demanded—prompted UFC President Dana White to call him "the father of mixed martial arts."

*   *   *

While Bruce Lee may be the metaphorical father of mixed martial arts, more realistic claims can be made by businessman Art Davie and martial arts teacher Rorion Gracie.

In the early 1990s, Davie was an executive working for an advertising firm. Sent on a research assignment to find out what was going on in the world of martial arts, he went into Gracie's Torrance, California, gym because he had heard that it was the epicenter of what was hot in southern California. What he saw being taught was Brazilian jiu-jitsu, a hybrid form of martial arts that was taking the West by storm.

Brazilian jiu-jitsu (BJJ) owes its existence to two men—one from Japan, the other from Brazil.

Born in the northern Japanese city of Hirosaki in 1878, Mitsuyo Maeda grew up wanting to be a sumo wrestler, as it was the most popular sport in his home region. But with a 5-foot-4 frame carrying about 140 pounds, Maeda had little hope of ever becoming a sumo. So when his parents sent him to Tokyo for college, he was eager to sign up for judo, because he had heard that's what the best fighters there did.

He was a devoted student, and when judo started to become popular in the West, he was one of three men invited by businessman Sam Hill to come to the United States in 1905 to demonstrate their prowess. At the time, Theodore Roosevelt was an avid judo practitioner and he convinced the U.S. Naval Academy to allow the Japanese contingent to try out for positions as wrestling coaches for the Academy's students. The judo masters had no problem with the first few men they faced (including the incumbent wrestling instructor), but lost the job when hulking All-American football center Harold Tipton literally threw the group's leader, Tsunejiro Tomita, out of the ring.

Maeda and his group would have more success on the rest of their tour of the United States and Cuba and even more in Europe. Maeda made a home in London and wrestled professionally with some level of success while augmenting his income by teaching judo to the locals. After he lost a much-publicized bout to American boxer Sam McVey, Maeda realized his time in London was over and headed south to Spain.

He hated Belgium and was lukewarm on France, but he really enjoyed himself in Spain, where he was welcomed with open arms. And it was there that he acquired the stage name Conde Koma (Count Koma), a reference to *komaru*, a Japanese word that can mean disturbed, agitated or even crazy.

In 1909, a group of Japanese judo masters including Maeda took a trip to Mexico, where wrestling has a long and storied history. Maeda offered a challenge—the equivalent of $50 (then a huge sum) to any man he couldn't put to the ground and $500 to any who could pin him. There is no record of anybody collecting. Maeda liked the New World and continued to wrestle in Mexico, and occasionally Cuba, while trying unsuccessfully to drum up interest in the United States.

In 1914, his traveling tour took him to Brazil. Almost immediately he became incredibly popular there and settled down in the northern city Belém do Pará, took a wife and the name Otávio Maeda. While his career as a performer was still going, he opened a business teaching judo to the locals. But he didn't call it judo. Instead, he called it jiu-jitsu, in honor of the forerunner of modern judo (itself developed by another undersized teen who was picked on, 99-pound Jigoro Kano). It proved a success, and jiu-jitsu became one of Brazil's most popular sports, especially in the region surrounding Belém.

Gastão Gracie was also a resident of Belém, his family having arrived there from Scotland in 1926. He ran a number of businesses, including one that helped immigrants become naturalized Brazilian citizens. Maeda was one of his clients, and the two men hit it off right away and became friends. In 1917, Gastão brought Carlos, aged 14 and the oldest of his five sons, to see Maeda fight. Carlos was astounded by what he saw and decided then and there to make jiu-jitsu his life's work. Carlos took lessons from Maeda and passed the knowledge on to his bothers Oswaldo, Gastão Jr., Jorge and Hélio.

The family moved to Rio de Janiero in 1921. Although they were no longer taught by Maeda, they continued their training on their own, and in 1925 Carlos opened his own training school. It proved relatively popular and attracted all kinds of clients, including some quite prominent ones.

One of those high-profile students was Bank of Brazil director Mario Brandt. Carlos was late for one lesson in 1928, so 16-year-old Hélio volunteered to step in. When Carlos arrived and apologized for being late, Brandt told him it was no problem and that he so impressed by Hélio and his different kind of jiu-jitsu that he wanted Hélio to be his own personal instructor.

Carlos taught something very close to the traditional judo Maeda performed. Judo is a grappling sport in which the aim is to subdue one's opponent by means of locking, twisting or throwing. There are strikes in judo, but they can only be used by higher-level practitioners for training purposes and never in competition.

That's fine for a big, strong guy like Carlos, but Hélio was much smaller. To keep up with and even best his many fighting brothers, Hélio had to develop his own style of fighting. Its basis was in traditional judo, but he added hand strikes taken from boxing and karate, and kicks borrowed from muay Thai (kickboxing) and karate. His new style of fighting became known as Gracie jiu-jitsu and eventually, Brazilian jiu-jitsu.

It and he became very popular. In fact, in 1935 four of the Gracies attacked a gymnastics coach named Manoel Rufino in front of dozens of his students. For his part in the assault, Hélio was sentenced to two-and-a-half years in prison, but was immediately pardoned by Brazilian president Getúlio Vargas against the express wishes of the Supreme Court. There were many rumors about why Vargas pardoned Hélio, but none were conclusively proven. Still, Hélio did teach Vargas's son Maneco years later.

The original Gracies were followed by dozens of others (Carlos himself had 21 children), many of whom found success in the family business. And BJJ probably would have stayed in Brazil if it hadn't been for a few coincidences.

Hélio had nine children—seven sons and two daughters—all of whom had first names starting with the letter R. All of them were involved in the family business, and one of them, the eldest Rorion, performed before audiences while still in diapers.

In 1969, 17-year-old Rorion traveled to the United States. After visiting relatives in New York City and Washington, D.C., he made a pilgrimage to Hollywood. He loved it and finally moved to southern California in 1978. He rented a small house in Torrance and supported himself doing work as an extra in movies and TV shows. He set up some mats in his garage and invited everyone he met for a free BJJ lesson. It took off. "Over the years, I always had people coming to my garage to fight," Rorion later said. "That happened almost as soon as I got to America." By 1985, Rorion had so many students that he recruited his 18-year-old brother Royce to come up from Brazil to be his assistant.

Rorion was working on a movie set when he was introduced to director Richard Donner. Donner, best known at that point in his career for *The Omen*, watched a short demonstration of BJJ and hired Rorion to choreograph the fight scenes for his next movie, *Lethal Weapon*. He became an overnight sensation in the American martial arts world, and was even profiled in *Playboy* magazine. Rorion produced a documentary, *Gracie Jiu-Jitsu in Action*, which showed members of the Gracie family (starting with Hélio) taking on and soundly defeating judo masters, kickboxers, karate champions and all kinds of other fighters in Brazilian exhibition matches. It was never released by a studio—instead being distributed by Rorion himself—but it caused a sensation in the martial arts community.

His star was rising. By the middle of 1989, he had clearly outgrown the garage. With 120 regular students and 80 more on the waiting list, Rorion opened a gym in Torrance, which is now referred to as the Gracie's "World Headquarters."

And it was that gym that Art Davie visited in 1991. Impressed by Rorion and BJJ, Davie became a member and quickly gained Rorion's trust by making him some money. "Rorion had done this videotape called *Gracies in Action*, which showed some of the mixed-style fights his family had done," Davie recalled. "I volunteered to do a direct-mail base for him. He didn't know what it was, but I convinced him to do it. He had 25,000 names in a database he had collected over the months and years. We did a mailing list and grossed over $100,000. So then I had credibility with him."

Davie then befriended another student, screenwriter and director John Milius—most famous for writing *Apocalypse Now* and directing *Conan the Barbarian*, but also known for being the model for John Goodman's Walter Sobchak character in the Coen brothers' film *The Big Lebowski*. The three of them would train and watch Rorion's videotapes of Brazilian *vale tudo* fighting.

Normally vale tudo is translated as "no holds barred" because it is basically without rules, but the literal translation is something closer to "to win everything," similar to the concept of "winner takes it all."

Vale tudo began in Brazilian traveling circuses, in which strong men would fight for money and would often challenge the locals to pin them or knock them out. Any type of fighting was allowed and foreign fighters with exotic techniques, especially those from east Asia, were considered a huge draw. But the best fighters were usually those who mixed their techniques and honed them through years of street fighting.

The sport's popularity peaked in 1959–60 when a TV show called *Heróis do Ringue* (Heroes of the Ring) aired in the Rio de Janeiro region. There were Gracies everywhere, serving as staff, hosts and competitors. The show was a great success, until one night in 1960 when João Alberto Barreto broke his opponent's arm on live TV. Shocked, the network cancelled the show. Even without widespread media coverage, vale tudo remained relatively popular, but had been tainted with an association to uncontrolled violence and went underground.

But Davie and Milius loved it. Their watching the videos started some pretty predictable conversations. The three men pondered a number of age-old questions: Could a boxer beat a wrestler? How about a karate champ against a judo master? Of course, it all culminated with the bigger question—what's the best of all fighting styles? And the even bigger, unspoken question—who is the best fighter in the world?

Under normal circumstances, three men posing such questions would not amount to much. But Rorion was a champ with many years of experience and generations of knowledge, and he was an entrepreneur who knew what he had to do to get his message across. Davie was a high-powered marketing man with contacts everywhere. And Milius—though universally regarded as eccentric—was among the most famous writers and directors in Hollywood. He had lots of valuable friends.

There had been plenty of exhibition matches pitting different styles of fighters before—often in Southeast Asia, Brazil and Mexico. Davie himself had seen a Thai boxer take on an Indian wrestler in Bangkok when he was in the Marines. But they wanted to put on something bigger, more definitive.

Davie came up with the plan. They would pit eight men—all from different fighting styles—against one another in a single-elimination tournament to determine who was the best fighter in the world. He even had a name—*War of the Worlds*. Rorion and Milius (who was named creative director) signed on and Davie immediately went to work making it happen. He showed his 65-page business plan to a number of potential investors (many of them Rorion's students) and got a $250,000 stake from 28 of them. He called the new company W.O.W. Promotions and began to negotiate for a television deal.

The owners of HBO and Showtime declined, calling the idea "crazy," but Davie did get a deal with New York City–based Semaphore Entertainment Group (SEG). The founder and president of SEG, Bob Meyrowitz, was well known at the time because of his syndicated radio show, *The King Biscuit Flower Hour*, and became one of the pioneers of pay-per-view television after broadcasting profitable performances by Whoopi Goldberg and Barbra Streisand. Meyrowitz was well known for taking chances and was just a few months removed from producing a very successful exhibition tennis match in Las Vegas between Jimmy Connors and

Martina Navratilova when Davie approached him early in 1993. It was agreed that W.O.W. would pay for the event and SEG would pay for the telecast, with the two companies splitting the revenue. It has been said that Meyrowitz's employee Michael Abramson came up with the name "Ultimate Fighting Championship."

They decided on McNichols Sports Arena in Denver as the venue. Right next to Mile High Stadium, McNichols (or "Big Mac" as it was known) had a 16,000–17,000 capacity and was then home to the NBA's Nuggets and the NHL's Avalanche. It wasn't their first choice. They wanted it to be in Brazil, but the logistical problems were huge and Meyrowitz wasn't sure American viewers would be that interested in a new event held in such an unfamiliar country.

Davie had done some homework and found out that Colorado was the only state in which bare-knuckle boxing was legal, there was no governing athletic commission *and* limited liability insurance for such events was legal and easy to acquire. He incorporated there and booked the arena.

The date was set for November 12, 1993. They lined up their on-camera talent. Kickboxers Bill "Superfoot" Wallace and Kathy "The Punisher" Long would team up with NFL-Hall-of-Famer Jim Brown for the play-by-play and future Fox News personality Brian Kilmeade provided fighter interviews. SEG took care of the pay-per-view. Rorion tried to recruit his friend Chuck Norris to be a commentator, but Norris had questions about the legality of the match and, although excited about its potential, could not even be persuaded to attend in person.

The competitors were harder to decide on, but mostly easy to recruit. The fighters were to be paid just $1,000 to appear and the winner of the tournament was to receive $50,000. Davie placed ads in martial arts magazines and wrote letters to major dojos around North America.

And, of course, there had to be a Gracie. While the stated purpose of the Ultimate Fighting Championship was to determine which discipline of fighting was the best, it was certainly in the best interest of the Gracies to showcase the family business at the same time. It has been widely reported that SEG had expressed a desire for Rickson Gracie—who was, at the time, the family's best and certainly toughest-looking fighter—but Rorion had a different plan. So confident was he that the Gracie school of BJJ would dominate any fight, he instead chose little brother Royce. At a thin 178 pounds and with a baby face, Royce didn't look like a badass. The sight of Royce beating up much bigger, stronger men added significantly more allure to the Gracie style of BJJ. And, potentially, more paying customers.

With the fighters in the fold, the next task was marketing. SEG's head of development, Campbell McLaren (sometimes referred to as the "brains behind the UFC") viewed the fight strictly as a one-off. "The last thing we want is for this to be a sport," he said. He was joined by colorful local promoter Zane "Insane Zane" Bresloff, who had to work in secret because his usual employer was the WWF.

After the elimination rounds, the championship match pitted Royce Gracie against Gerard Gordeau, a tall (6-foot-5) rangy Dutchman. In addition to a bandage on his hand, Gordeau had another on his right foot, covering wounds from an earlier bout in which two of his opponent's teeth were embedded in his instep, while others flew into the crowd. Seconds after the bell rang, Royce went in for the shoot. Gordeau didn't fall for it and stayed on his feet. Royce grappled with him and locked his right foot behind Gordeau's left leg. The two limped to the fence together, Royce put his arms around the big man and finally took him down. On the bottom, Gordeau was trying to find a hold when he received two nasty head butts. Gordeau broke Royce's hold and rolled over on his belly. But that gave Royce an opportunity to get his left arm under his opponent's throat. Gordeau, in incredible pain and in danger of passing out, knew he had no recourse. He tapped out. Little Royce Gracie had won the Ultimate Fighting Championship.

No noteworthy commentator has ever accused the UFC's organizers of fixing the event (and there is no evidence they did), but it could not have worked out better for the Gracies. Not only did David slay a number of Goliaths, but the sling he used was nothing other than Gracie BJJ.

If you had been at the Big Mac that night, you might not have seen what a success *UFC 1* was. After all, the 2,800 fans there may have been excited (there was even a small riot in the stands at one point), but they were vastly outnumbered by empty seats. But far more important were the 86,000 pay-per-view subscriptions SEG sold, not to mention the numerous VHS cassettes and the incredible amount of good publicity the Gracies' BJJ school received. The original investors saw a return in revenue of at least seven times what they put in.

They had proved McLaren wrong. They had made a sport of it. Just a few months later, *UFC 1* was followed by *UFC 2* on March 11, 1994. Also staged in Denver—but at the more appropriate 3,700-seat Mammoth Events Center (now called the Fillmore Auditorium)—the event drew just 2,000 fans. But SEG sold an incredible 300,000 pay-per-view licenses. What had been a one-off idea by a bunch of California-based martial arts fans had morphed into a multimillion-dollar industry—and a burgeoning sport. And since Royce won again, the worldwide reputation of the Gracies and their brand of BJJ kept growing.

But things began to change. Many in the martial arts world noticed Royce's success and began to emulate his style. But periods of slow action in the fights turned off many viewers and the number of pay-per-view customers began to decline sharply. To combat this, the UFC instituted time limits for the matches. But there was a problem. Without judges, there was no way to declare a winner if a fight reached the time limit.

And on April 7, 1995, at *UFC 5* in Charlotte, North Carolina, the worst-case scenario occurred. A long-awaited rematch from *UFC 1* between Royce Gracie and Georgia-born Ken Shamrock saw the pair go at it for what seemed like forever without any discernable action, never mind a conclusive winner. The crowd was alive with boos, and even Shamrock's second—his own father, Bob Shamrock—was shouting at him to "do something!" After an excruciating-to-watch 31 minutes, the event's referee, John "Big John" McCarthy, stepped in and separated the pair. After a five-minute break, they restarted. But after another five minutes of grappling, with the crowd booing lustily, McCarthy stepped in again and ended the fight, declaring it a draw. *UFC 5* was instead won by Dan "The Beast" Severn whose kimura forced fellow wrestler Dave Beneteau to submit.

It was a turning point for the UFC, and the desire for new rules and the inclusion of judges proved decisive. Rorion was said to be angry that the new-look UFC would be a diluted version of what he had originally envisioned, and he divested himself of the organization. Davie also sold his share—leaving SEG as the UFC's sole owner as Milius had only invested in the first event—but stayed on as the league's commissioner until the end of 1997.

Things were looking up for the fledgling organization, despite the loss of the Gracies. Mixed martial arts had become popular nationwide and, even though they had dropped, pay-per-view licences were still running at up to 260,000 per event and VHS sales were strong. More money and more exposure led to a better class of fighter, which in turn made the league even more popular.

But there would be a barrier to success. Known now for his 2008 run as the Republican presidential candidate who lost to Barack Obama, John McCain had been in Arizona government since 1983, and was a well-respected senior senator when he was sent some VHS tapes of UFC events. A lifelong boxing fan, McCain was shocked by the uncontrolled violence in the Octagon. He made it a personal campaign to wipe it from the face of the Earth. He personally wrote impassioned letters to the legislatures of all 50 U.S. states and 10 Canadian provinces imploring them to outlaw the sport. He called it "repugnant" and famously referred to it as "human cockfighting."

It worked surprisingly well. Before long, exhibitions of mixed martial arts competitions were banned in 36 states and seven provinces. He also used his connections at the Federal Communications Commission (FCC) to contact pay-per-view distributors to convince them not to carry UFC events. That worked, too. SEG's main distributor, Viewer's Choice, and many smaller carriers dropped the UFC.

One of the states that outlawed the UFC was New York. That posed a problem: *UFC 12* was set to be held in New York City. It was a huge blow because a show in Manhattan would be a big boost to the sport's national and international recognition. Frantically, the organizers looked for an alternate venue. They settled on one in Portland, Oregon, only to be rebuffed when that state also refused to sanction the event. Finally they settled on Dothan, Alabama—a 65,000-person dot on the map that calls itself "The Peanut Capital of the World."

The event itself was different. As a nod to fans who were tired of seeing 175-pound martial artists take on 400-pound behemoths, weight classes were established. It was crude—participants over 200 pounds were heavyweights, those under were lightweights—but it was a sign that the UFC was willing to make adjustments to keep fan interest. It also marked the beginning of the UFC's association with popular comedian Joe Rogan.

But it was a tough time for the league. Although 3,100 people attended the event (selling out the Dothan Civic Center), the pay-per-view audience was limited, with only then-small DirecTV carrying the event. Although no reliable numbers regarding the pay-per-view audience were ever made public, most experts agree that the number was not far from 25,000. *UFC 12* marked the beginning of what some fans call the "Underground Era" or even the "Dark Ages" of the UFC, during which the league held events in the few states without sanctioning bodies, in Japan and in Brazil. The live crowds were enthusiastic but the pay-per-view audiences were tiny. Even finding distributors for the videotapes proved increasingly tough.

Desperate to end the marginalization of their sport, UFC officials met with state athletic commissions and let it be known that they were willing to make big changes if it meant that their product could get sanctioning. Although the Gracies, Davie and Milius probably would have disapproved, the UFC began to institute a number of rules and more weight classes. Responding to criticisms about fighter safety, the UFC instituted gloves as mandatory equipment and eliminated kicks to the head of a downed opponent, hair pulling, fish-hooking (inserting fingers into the mouth or nostril of an opponent), head butts and strikes to the groin. That was followed by bans on strikes to the back of the neck and head as well as small joint manipulation, such as the twisting of fingers and toes.

Surprisingly, it was another mixed martial arts organization— the much smaller International Fighting Championships (IFC), which was based in the United States but held its first event in Kiev, Ukraine—that first achieved sanctioning in the United States. It happened in Mississippi in 1996. But it didn't mean much to the

UFC because it was already holding events in states very much like Mississippi without the need for sanctioning. It wasn't until the IFC was sanctioned in New Jersey on September 30, 2000, that the UFC really took notice. Not only is New Jersey home to nearly 9 million relatively affluent Americans, but it's well within the New York City communications universe. Acting quickly, the UFC adopted New Jersey's "unified rules of mixed martial arts," which had been developed by the IFC, and set up an event in the Garden State.

Set at the Trump Taj Mahal Casino Hotel in Atlantic City on November 17, 2000, *UFC 28* marked the beginning of a new era for the UFC. Gis and any clothes other than trunks and the now-mandatory gloves and shoes were banned. Rounds lasted five minutes and were judged. If no fighter submitted or was knocked out after five rounds, the judges would declare a winner. Even McCain, once the UFC's greatest opponent, changed his mind. "The sport has grown up," he told a British newspaper. "The rules have been adopted to give its athletes better protections and to ensure fairer competition."

It worked. To some extent. *UFC 28* sold all 5,000 tickets, but the pay-per-view audience was still minuscule. And, as a result, SEG was facing bankruptcy. Dana White, a former aerobics instructor who managed two prominent UFC fighters (Tito Ortiz and Chuck Liddell) at the time, caught wind that SEG was looking for a buyer for the UFC, so he called his old friend Lorenzo Fertitta, who co-owned Station Casinos with his brother Frank and had previously been Nevada's state athletic commissioner. The Fertittas put together a company called Zuffa, LLC, bought the UFC, gave White a 10 percent share and named him president.

Zuffa put a lot of money into the UFC, increasing advertising, promotion and DVD distribution. And they worked very closely with state and provincial authorities in an effort to gain more widespread acceptance of their product. After that, the UFC began to come back.

And by the time GSP made his debut in *UFC 46* in Las Vegas on January 31, 2004, the Dark Ages were well and truly over. Mixed martial arts had eclipsed boxing as North America's martial art of choice and professional wrestling as its most popular combat sport. Held at the Mandalay Bay Events Center, *UFC 46* had 10,700 spectators for a claimed gate of $1,377,000 and a pay-per-view audience of 80,000.

The UFC had established itself as a major sport. And it was looking for a hero.

CHAPTER 2

To understand GSP, you have to know his roots. You'll often hear he's from Montreal, but he is actually from a small town about 20 miles to the south called Saint-Isidore.

There are at least three places called Saint-Isidore in Quebec, but GSP's home town is on what Montrealers call the South Shore. That region, officially called the Roussillon Regional Municipality, encompasses the territory south of the island of Montreal on the banks of the St. Lawrence River, except for a roughly triangular chunk of land known as the Kahnawake Mohawk Territory. Anchored by the pleasant suburb of Châteauguay on its western end, Roussillon is primarily made up of small bedroom communities, old villages and farmland.

Saint-Isidore is a far cry from the busy and diverse streets of Montreal. Dominated by a limestone quarry that provided the raw material to build churches and pave roads for generations, the town is surrounded by the dairy, corn and pork farms endemic to the region. About 95 percent of its inhabitants speak French at home, and the area is considered a safe seat for the federalist Bloc Québécois party in federal elections.

These days you'll see a lot of new prefabricated-looking houses, as the population—now at about 2,700—has been growing rapidly for the past few years. High prices and congestion have worked to move people out of Montreal and into the suburbs. And since Saint-Isidore is just 25 minutes or so down Route 207 (also known as Rue Saint-Isidore) from the Honoré Mercier Bridge, which connects the South Shore to the Montreal borough of LaSalle, it has become an increasingly attractive place for families to relocate. (It's still small, though. When I went there to speak with residents about GSP and his childhood, I was surprised to see a horse in one family's front yard.)

And Saint-Isidore was not always a commuter town. Just a few years ago, it was much smaller and much quieter. It was one of those places with only one of everything—one doctor, one dentist, one lawyer—in which everybody knew everybody else and most of their business.

It was in this village that Roland and Paulyne St-Pierre introduced their first child, Georges, on May 19, 1981. The St-Pierres were not a wealthy family by any means. Roland worked in flooring and Paulyne was a night-shift caregiver for the elderly. But they were proud, honest and hard-working people, and they instilled many of those qualities in little Georges from an early age. "We didn't have a lot of money, but I always ate my three meals a day," Georges told a reporter years later. "I grew up with the mentality that I had to work to get what I want. I'm glad in a certain way. My parents helped me financially but they never gave me something for free . . . it's probably the best gift they ever gave me."

From a young age, it was clear that Georges was different from many of the other kids in the area. He was small, but he had an independent, even stubborn, streak about him, which could sometimes rub his peers the wrong way. "Georges was different in the way he thought and acted, not a nerd, but kind of hyperactive," said Gerardo Lanctôt, one of his oldest friends. "He was a bit marginalized."

Actually, it was worse than that. Almost as soon as he arrived at school, Georges was a target for bullies. "I went to a school where it was pretty rough," he has said. "I'd get my clothes stolen, my cash." Considering how terrible the South Shore winters can be, this conjures up a sad image of six-year-old Georges waiting for the school bus without a coat, hat, mittens or boots. Things could get physical, too, but little Georges wouldn't give up anything without a fight. "Even though I knew I was going to get beat up when somebody was trying to steal my lunch money," he said, "I always fought for it." Still, his young age, small size and lack of anyone to stand up for him meant he didn't stand a chance against the bigger boys. "I got my ass kicked a lot of times in the street at this time. A lot of people ask me: 'Hey, Georges, you must be undefeated in the street; I think that nobody can beat you,'" he has recalled. "That may be now, but when I was young, I think my record was two victories and 25 losses . . . when you are eight [or] nine years old and the other guys are 12 [or] 13, they are teenagers and you are a kid." As he grew stronger, he would sometimes be set upon by as many as five guys at once.

There was little respite once he got home. "I grew up with a lot of anger," he once recalled. "In my school it was bad, and in my house it was bad." He has never elaborated on what was bad at home in his early years, but it appears to have now been forgotten or at least forgiven. Not only is Georges close with his parents and siblings these days, he even paid off his parents' mortgage with some of the undisclosed amount of money he earned defeating Jon Fitch at *UFC 87: Seek and Destroy* in Minneapolis on August 9, 2008.

Despite his small size, Georges excelled at sports from a very young age. He liked track and field and basketball, but was particularly fond of hockey. In fact, he loved it. And in a perfect example of his independent, almost contrarian, nature, he was a devoted fan of the Edmonton Oilers. That was almost blasphemy on the South Shore, where being a fan of the *rouge-blanc-et-bleu* of *Les Habitants* (or the Habs, as the Montréal Canadiens are known there) was as vital a part of growing up as eating or sleeping. When Georges was not old enough to watch the Oilers play on TV—Edmonton is in the Mountain time zone and Oilers games start two hours later than those in Montreal—but the Oilers were playing in the Stanley Cup finals, his father (himself a fan of the much-despised-on-the-South-Shore Quebec Nordiques) would wake him up to watch the celebrations.

But the amount of equipment needed for hockey can be quite expensive, even if used gear is purchased. Add ice time and transportation, and hockey becomes a very costly investment. It was more than the St-Pierres could afford. With two little girls in the house—Georges has two sisters, one three years younger than him, the other five years younger—there just wasn't always enough time or money left over for hockey.

It was a familiar situation for the St-Pierre family. Georges' father, Roland, had been a promising athlete, but he had to cut his dreams short when his father died. He had to get a job to support his family. But he did continue with a less expensive sport—kyokushin karate. In fact, he earned a black belt. He realized that with karate he could fulfill Georges' interest in sports and also teach him to defend himself at the same time. So Roland started instructing his son when he was just seven years old. By the time he was nine, Georges was very good. There was room in the family budget to enroll him in a nearby karate school and even to let him play a little hockey. "My parents were very good with me; they wanted to keep me in sports because they didn't want me to hang out with bad people and become a criminal or anything like that," he recalled. "I was in a very tough school; my childhood wasn't easy."

Today, many fighters and some fight fans often dismiss karate as more a means of demonstration than of actual fighting. The world of mixed martial arts has shown that grappling and wrestling are far more effective at dominating an opponent than the stylized punches and kicks of karate, and is rarely used in the UFC anymore. Georges was lucky enough to enroll with an instructor, Jean Couture, who taught the kyokushinkai-kan style of karate.

Developed in 1964 by Masutatsu Oyama (who was born Choi Young-Eui in Korea, but later became a naturalized Japanese citizen), kyokushin—which can be translated as "ultimate truth"—is centered less around tradition, and more around moves that help in real-world fighting situations. It's one of the few derivatives of karate that incorporates some grappling techniques.

Georges was outstanding in his training. He mastered the discipline easily and went through belts rapidly. But when he was 12, his parents gave him a choice; he had to decide between hockey and karate. They simply couldn't afford both. As has become obvious since, Georges chose karate. "I liked karate better because hockey is a team sport and in karate, like any other martial art, you're alone. You decide your own destiny," he explained. "Sometimes when you play hockey, you play very well but your teammates don't, so it messes up everything." And, by his own admission, he was not an outstanding hockey player.

Unburdened by teammates, Georges focused on karate and chess. At the age of 13, he earned Nidan (second-degree black belt) status and was also named one of the top 25 young chess players in Quebec. But when Jean Couture died of lung cancer, his karate training was interrupted. He later said that he was so sad, he almost quit. Luckily he found a dojo that taught muay Thai. "I don't want to say this, as it is not a good thing, but when he died I started a new style of martial arts," he recalled later. "That he died made me start my career in MMA."

At that time, Georges and some friends did something that changed the course of his life. Looking for something to do, they went to the town convenience store to rent a video. They found a copy of *UFC 1: The Beginning*, by then a couple of years old. Georges was transfixed, impressed that Royce Gracie could dominate men much bigger than him, and he saw that the way to win a real fight was to incorporate grappling, not just striking. "When I first saw [Gracie] fight, I did not know what . . . Brazilian jiu-jitsu [was]," he recalled years later. "Grappling was unknown in Quebec, where I come from. Everybody thought that a fight was standing up, and it was mostly like what they show in the movies à la Jean-Claude Van Damme. But Royce Gracie made me realize the truth, the reality, and he inspired me also because he was fighting guys who were, like, twice his size. And he was beating them all . . . without any damage."

Not only did young Georges see that a smaller fighter like Gracie could easily defeat much bigger men, but he also saw that the way he had been taught to fight wasn't the only way to defeat an opponent.

Georges figured out that he had to learn how to fight like a Gracie, but there was a problem—there were not any Brazilian jiu-jitsu dojos on the South Shore or in Montreal at that time. "I liked muay Thai, but then I saw the first Ultimate Fighting Championship with Ken Shamrock, and those guys inspired me to become a mixed martial arts fighter," he has said. "As soon as I saw the UFC, I wanted to train for it, but at that time jiu-jitsu didn't exist in Montreal. I decided to train in muay Thai, and later on I got my third-degree black belt in karate."

It was at about that time when Georges missed his first opportunity to see a live professional mixed martial arts fight. The fledgling International Fighting Championships (IFC) had held one successful fight in the Ukraine, and another upstart organization called Battlecade Extreme Fighting (BEF) was looking for a big North American venue to raise the stakes. BEF had already held an event in Wilmington, North Carolina, but failed to get a major pay-per-view deal and had sold few videocassettes. It made plans to hold a second match in the New York area in hopes of raising the BEF's profile, but the state government declared it, and what state officials called "no holds barred" fighting, illegal. Desperate for a quick replacement, Battlecade officials made a controversial decision to stage the event at the Kahnawake Mohawk reserve. The date for *Battlecade: Extreme Fighting 2* was set for Friday, April 26, 1996.

As was usual at the time, the idea of a professional mixed martial arts fight caused an uproar in parts of the community and, especially, the media. It certainly didn't help that the promoters billed it as "the most brutal event in the history of the sport."

The Quebec premier at the time, Lucien Bouchard, described the event as illegal, said that he expected the Kahnawake Peacekeepers (an internal Mohawk police force funded by the provincial government) to put a stop to it and asked the federal government to block any pay-per-view transmissions.

The Mohawks contended that *Extreme Fighting 2* was not technically prizefighting because there was no actual purse to be won (the fighters were to receive pre-determined payouts) and that the fighters were all going to wear regulation 5-ounce gloves. The province countered by pointing out that any organized fight without the sanction of a recognized governing body was illegal, no matter what the minor details were.

Naturally, 14-year-old Georges was desperate to go. Mixed martial arts was almost unknown in Canada, but he knew what it was. Roland had no problem with the idea, but Paulyne forbade her son to attend. Her problem wasn't the brutality of exhibition itself, the government's opposition or the potentially dangerous crowd; instead, it stemmed from the fact that one of the event's sponsors was *Penthouse* magazine (the company that publishes *Penthouse* owned Battlecade), and so she declared the event unsuitable for her young son.

The provincial government got a last-minute injunction that prevented Canadian media giant Bell from broadcasting the event for pay-per-view audiences, so the organizers rented a broadcast van from a TV station in Portland, Maine, and rigged up its own feed.

With ticket prices ranging from $200 for ringside seats to $20 for standing-room only, *Extreme Fighting 2* drew an enthusiastic crowd of over 4,000. It started at 9:05 when six *Penthouse* models took to the ring in swimsuits to greet the crowd. Then the announcer assumed center stage and the action was on. There were six fights, including one 44-second match in which 159-pound Ralph "Pitbull" Gracie (a first cousin of Rorion and Royce) easily defeated a much bigger fighter named Steve Nelson. The whole show went off without any major incidents—until the next day, that is.

On Saturday, 12 officers from the Sûreté du Quebec (SQ, the Quebec provincial police) and three peacekeepers from the Kahnawake Mohawk Nation descended upon the Hôtel du Parc and arrested five fighters who had spent the night there, the referee, and the announcer, and issued warrants for others involved.

Nelson later said that the cops busted in on him and his girlfriend, Mitzi Jones, who were both nude at the time, watching TV. He claimed that the police ignored her pleas to get dressed while they arrested him. The entire group was held in jail and finally released after arraignment on Monday.

The arrests were greeted with shock and dismay by many in the mixed martial arts community. "At the beginning here, you had the drama of trying to do ultimate combat on the Indian reserve, and then bang, it's illegal; 'We're going to arrest fighters, we're going to this, we're going to that,'" said Shawn Mozen, a Montreal-based mixed martial arts trainer and commentator. "And it's really given what is a very impressive sport—where you meet guys like Georges and [fellow Montreal-based fighter] David ["The Crow" Loiseau] who are true gentlemen—a bad name."

The province's swift action restarted a heated debate with the Mohawks about their sovereignty. Kahnawake Chief Joe Norton furiously called the injunction a "double-cross," and threatened to further chill the already frosty relations with the provincial government—which had been particularly stressed since the 1990 Oka Crisis, which left one police officer dead— after the arrests. Eventually, all charges were dropped and the Quebec government—suddenly aware of which way the wind was blowing—moved to sanction mixed martial arts matches in the province. Governed by similar rules to those that began in New Jersey, mixed martial arts became legal in Quebec in 1998.

The Kahnawake Mohawks would continue to host IFC events, beginning with *IFC: Cage Combat* in May 1998. And 16-year-old Georges was there. He had his mother's permission, if not exactly her blessing. "I felt guilty," she said. "Why did he need to be a part of so much violence? What did I do wrong?" But Georges assured her that he wasn't into the sport because of the violence, but because of the athleticism and the strategy.

He saw 10 matches that night, with a wide variety of styles. It got a little ugly when Miguel "The Ripper" Menendez was disqualified for illegally head-butting Brazilian-style jiu-jitsu fighter Jay Russell, but the event was generally regarded as a decent show. Most of the fighters were relative unknowns at the time. The headline match saw Belarusian wrestler Vladimir "The Janitor" Matyushenko score a TKO against muay Thai fighter Anthony "Mad Dog" Macias in just 16 seconds.

Georges was, by this time, totally hooked. He graduated high school—bullies long-since a memory—and enrolled at CÉGEP, a type of junior college endemic to Quebec. His English-speaking skills began to improve.

It was a busy time for him. He still did some karate, earning a third-degree (Sandan) black belt; he had found a competent Brazilian jiu-jitsu teacher and had also taken up both boxing and wrestling. He was a good student at Collège Édouard-Montpetit in Longueuil, earning a diploma in natural science and a technical diploma in flooring. Besides his training and his school work, he worked four different jobs and was lucky to get five hours of sleep a night. Wisely, he trained in as many different styles as he could, working on boxing one day and Brazilian jiu-jitsu the next.

He was also fighting amateur mixed martial arts on the side. "I won my first amateur [mixed martial arts] fight," he said. "I was 16 years old, and I defeated a guy [who] was 25." Georges easily won his fight by knockout, taking his opponent down with a swift roundhouse kick to the head, but the fight also taught him how much he still had to learn. "I was merely a kyokushin karate fighter [at the time] and the guy I fought was a boxer," he said. "At that point my ground skills weren't the best; I had no idea about ground work." Had he drawn just about any other type of fighter, he could have run into serious trouble.

He did his best to keep his fights in the ring, even though he was by then well aware that he could easily dispose of any of the self-styled bad guys he'd run into on the South Shore. But it wasn't always possible to calm every situation with words. When asked years later about his last fight outside the ring, GSP recalled:

> It was when I was 17 years old, and I was . . . trying to get out of a nightclub because somebody was picking on me—a guy of, like, 25 years old. And . . . I was outside. And he was following me outside, and he was [going to] hit me with a bottle of beer. So I didn't have a choice to defend myself. I end[ed] up [breaking] his arm. But I was on mount position on top of him, and I just, like, showed him my fist to make him understand that if I wanted to hit him more and to cause a lot more damage, I could have done it. I let him go away without any cerebral damage or any bad things.

He used his technical diploma and the knowledge his father had imparted to him to land a job at a carpet store, and he used his athleticism to help instruct youth sports programs at a government-operated recreation center. He even had a brief stint as a garbage man. But the job from this period of his life that would be the most memorable was as a bouncer at a nearby nightclub called Fuzzy Brossard.

Despite its suburban South Shore setting and location in a strip mall beside a chain breakfast restaurant, Fuzzy Brossard is quite the nightspot. It can accommodate up to 1,000 partiers, mostly young professionals, and has played host to such notable acts as Timbaland, Akon, Fat Joe and Sean Paul.

One Fuzzy Brossard habitué, Longueuil native Conrad Ricard, told me that he remembered seeing Georges serve as a bouncer there. "It was funny to see him; when you think of a club bouncer, you think of some big biker type or a giant black dude, and here was this little guy," he said. "Don't get me wrong, you could tell he was fit and plenty tough, but he didn't look like [how] you would picture a bouncer." Ricard told me he had seen Georges escort drunks from the bar, but couldn't recall an incident where Georges had to resort to violence.

For his part, Georges remembered that using his wit and charm worked much better than the threat of violence. He told a reporter a story that encapsulated how he put his philosophy into action:

> To be a bouncer at this place, I was probably one of the smallest guys, so I had to use my brain. In the street you can be as strong as you want, but nobody's faster than a bullet. Being a bouncer, according to me, it's more being able to talk and being able to use words instead of your arms to do the job. One time I had a problem with some-body, and I was like: "Hey come outside. I need to talk you. The music is too loud [inside]." And once we were outside, [I said] "Sorry, my friend; you hit on every girl, you make trouble, you grab the girls' asses. Tonight you're finished. You can come back tomorrow, I don't mind. It's nothing personal, but tonight is over." [Then he replied], "Oh, you have no right to kick me out, you . . ." and I just said, "Bye-bye, have a good night."

The drunk in question knew better than to challenge him.

A big part of his ability to avoid fights in the nightclub stemmed from his reputation as an undefeated amateur fighter. "I never had problems with guys while bouncing. Some people know me and when they do know who I am, they respect me and I respect them. One person came up to me and said: 'Hey, I heard you are a fighter. Hey, me too. When I was young, I did kung fu. What do I have to do to do this job?' I saw the guy had a beer in one hand and he smoked weed. So I said to the guy, 'First you have to stop drinking and then stop smoking.'"

But the potential for violence at the club eventually got to him. He left the job as soon as he could. "I remember the day that I quit the club. I was telling everybody, 'Hey, if you keep acting like that [being rough with gang members], one day somebody's going to get shot,'" he recalled. "Two weeks after, there was a shootout at the club and somebody got shot. They tried to shoot the head door-man and they missed and they shot someone in the lineup in the leg."

Georges moved back home and continued to work, to work out and to fight as an amateur. These were small-time bouts in front of few people. But they weren't the goal, just a means. He wanted to be a fighter, a great fighter. All he needed was a chance.

CHAPTER

Once mixed martial arts fighting became a legal sport in Quebec, it was only a matter of time before a star amateur fighter like Georges got his chance. But even by the year 2000, while mixed martial arts was becoming a lucrative business, it remained marginalized in Canada.

But Montreal accepted mixed martial arts quickly. The tough neighborhoods in the area (particularly those downtown and on the South Shore) have long bred young men interested in fighting, and Montreal has a long and storied history of boxing—including the notorious Hilton family—and wrestling.

In fact, on November 9, 1997, Montreal was the center of pro wrestling attention. During the so-called "Montreal Screwjob," WWF owner Vince McMahon informed, privately and separately, both champion Bret "The Hit Man" Hart and challenger Shawn Michaels that the match decision would be in their favor. Then he informed the referees to declare Michaels the winner as soon as he had pinned Hart. That McMahon had fixed the fight drew worldwide attention and changed the way the WWF promoted its shows. The show had sold out the 20,000-seat Molson Centre (now known as the Bell Centre) and was very popular in the area as a pay-per-view event. At the time, only the Habs had more fans in Montreal than professional wrestling.

But by the turn of the millennium, interest in both boxing—with its tragic injuries and connections with crime—and professional wrestling—with its childishness and pre-determined results—was waning. It might not have if there hadn't been an alternative. But since mixed martial arts was by that time a legal, sanctioned competition in the region, Montrealers began to take to the newly recognized sport very quickly.

Although the UFC was slow to recognize Quebec as a market, for the IFC it had become something of a second home. Between its first truly legal Canadian match—*IFC 7: Cage Combat* on May 30, 1998, which Georges attended—and the summer of 2000, the IFC put on 11 events, and five of them were in the Montreal area (four at the Kahnawake Sports Complex and one at the Centre Pierre-Charbonneau in the city's rough-and-tumble Hochelaga-Maisonneuve neighborhood). All of them sold out.

Watching that kind of success, it was only a matter of time before local organizers got together and made their own series of events. The brainchild of local businessman Stephane Patry, the Universal Combat Challenge (UCC, later known as TKO Major League MMA or, more commonly, TKO) organized professional mixed martial arts matches in and around Montreal.

It was the first noteworthy Canadian mixed martial arts promotion company and it drew primarily from the ranks of local fighters. Despite the fact that many of their fighters and almost all their live-event spectators were French-Canadian, the UCC used English as its primary language in hopes of drawing a wider audience for future pay-per-view broadcasts and DVD sales.

Early events relied heavily on the star power of two talented Canadian fighters: David "The Crow" Loiseau and Justin "Loaf" Bruckmann. Loiseau, a taekwondo and muay Thai expert, was particularly popular, as he grew up in Montreal after his family arrived from Haiti when he was 10 years old. Loiseau would later become one of GSP's best friends and sparring partners.

Bruckmann was from Brooklin, Ontario (a rural village northeast of Toronto that is centered around a concrete factory), and his speciality was judo. Despite the size difference—Loiseau fought at about 185 pounds, Bruckmann at 155—they were pitted against each other in both of UCC's first two events. Bruckmann prevailed in the pair's first match at *UCC 1: The New Beginning*— forcing Loiseau to submit in three minutes and four seconds with a painful arm bar—but Loiseau avenged that loss with a guillotine choke that caused Bruckmann to submit three minutes and seven seconds into their second match at *UCC 2: The Moment of Truth* on August 12, 2000.

The community of mixed martial arts fighters and promoters was still fairly small and tight-knit at that point, and it wasn't long before the UCC came to see the much-talked-about undefeated amateur phenomenon named Georges St-Pierre. And their initial excitement was reciprocal. "When I first met Stephane Patry and his team, I decided I wanted to become a champion in this sport," St-Pierre later recalled.

They planned to have Georges make his debut at *UCC 7: Bad Boyz* set for January 25, 2002, at the Auditorium de Verdun in south Montreal. He was 20 years old. Despite the number in the event's title, *UCC 7* was the ninth mixed martial arts competition put on by the company. Five UCC main events were staged in either Montreal or Sherbrooke and one was put on in Quebec City. In addition, two UCC "Proving Ground" events (a kind of minor-league version of their main fights) had taken place at the Hôtel Saint-Jean-sur-Richelieu Gouverneur about 30 miles south of Montreal.

In his first pro fight, Georges was matched against Ivan "The Pride of El Salvador" Menjivar. A relatively small fighter at 5-foot-6 who usually fights at about 135 pounds, Menjivar was still a very tough first opponent. A seasoned practitioner of Brazilian jiu-jitsu, boxing, muay Thai and wrestling, Menjivar was an accomplished fighter who regularly dispatched much bigger opponents with what looked like ease.

Based in Montreal since he and his parents arrived from El Salvador when he was 12, Menjivar had a 4–0 record in UCC action, with two submissions and a TKO. His last fight—at *UCC Proving Ground 2* on December 16, 2001—saw him dispose of larger Dany Ward, a fellow Montrealer, in just over a minute with a flurry of punches. Small he may have been, but few would deny Menjivar was an extremely dangerous opponent for any fighter, let alone one making his professional debut. And, unlike any of St-Pierre's previous opponents, Menjivar was something of an expert when it came to the ground game (what observers still considered the weakest part of St-Pierre's own repertoire).

The bout's announcer described St-Pierre as an exciting young fighter making his UCC debut and pronounced his name in English as "George Saint Pierre." After demonstrating some quick punches and high kicks, St-Pierre addressed the camera in French. He introduced himself and said, "Outside the ring, I'm a gentleman, but what you see tonight inside the UCC ring . . . it's something else." Then he kissed his fist and aimed a punch at the camera lens.

As St-Pierre readied himself for the fight, the announcer introduced him first in English and then in French. He weighed in at 168 pounds. Menjivar, his ear taped from the Ward fight five weeks earlier, weighed in at 172 pounds, and was wide and thick with muscle. Because the UCC's cutoff point for a true welterweight was 169.9 pounds, league rules obligated Menjivar to surrender 20 percent of his purse to St-Pierre, win or lose, for being overweight. During the introductions, Menjivar smiled and gave St-Pierre a friendly salute.

It would be the third fight of the night, following two less-than-thrilling decisions. It began as tradition dictated, with the two fighters tapping gloves as a show of mutual respect. Then St-Pierre landed the first blow, a right kick to Menjivar's left hip. He then used his reach to plant a left hook to Menjivar's face. It put Menjivar off balance, but he lunged forward and managed to exchange a quick series of punches with St-Pierre. With a great deal of forward momentum favoring him, Menjivar used his much lower center of gravity to get under St-Pierre's flying fists and back him up. Just before they hit the ropes, Menjivar began lifting St-Pierre off his feet.

But the rookie recovered and spun him around. St-Pierre managed to push Menjivar backward and free himself from the ropes. He then landed a quick right to the abdomen and managed to break Menjivar's grasp. He paid for it with a quick right jab to the face, but at least he had gained a little bit of separation. Then, with a small hop that may have been a kick feint, St-Pierre moved in on the reeling Menjivar and unleashed two quick punches.

Up against the turnbuckle, Menjivar managed to lift St-Pierre off the mat and onto his shoulder. Flailing, St-Pierre managed to get his feet back on the ground and the two were clinched up against the ropes once again. Menjivar attempted to flip him over, but instead just pushed him into the ropes. That allowed St-Pierre to stand up with the help of the turnbuckle. Choosing to separate to give himself a chance to assess the situation, Menjivar landed a few punches and went back into the clinch. Holding the ropes to keep from going all the way down, St-Pierre landed in a sitting position and got up on all fours.

Sensing Menjivar going for a traditional wrestling takedown, St-Pierre spun onto his back and got his legs around Menjivar's waist. That allowed Menjivar—still on his feet and leaning over—to land a series of barely contested punches until St-Pierre got his hands behind his neck and pulled him down. With St-Pierre on the bottom, protecting his body with a butterfly guard, the two exchanged light punches and jockeyed for position. With 2:59 left in the five-minute round, the referee stepped in and broke them up.

St-Pierre then went for a single-leg takedown. Menjivar fought off his first couple of tries, but went down on the third. Menjivar went down on his back and St-Pierre immediately mounted him. Desperate, Menjivar wrapped his legs around his opponent's waist in an attempt to limit his ability to get at his upper body. St-Pierre hammered Menjivar's face with a couple of heavy lefts delivered from above. But St-Pierre appeared to put too much into his punches, and Menjivar managed to get his left leg free. Realizing he couldn't get Menjivar back into a vulnerable position again, St-Pierre let him get back up.

With a minute left, St-Pierre found himself on his back, just barely holding Menjivar off. While Menjivar was hammering small punches down on his face, St-Pierre managed to pry him off his body and got onto his feet.

With both of them standing, St-Pierre looked wobbly and in trouble against the ropes when he landed a soft right that caused Menjivar to slip backward. St-Pierre was now on top, in a much better position, and was raining hard punches down on his opponent. The ref jumped in to stop the action. There was some mouthing between the fighters and the ref, but it was clearly over.

At 4 minutes and 59 seconds into the five-minute fight, it was over. The referee determined that Menjivar had verbally tapped out. St-Pierre had won his first professional fight. It went in the books as a TKO at 4:50. St-Pierre was credited with 17 landed strikes and one takedown, and Menjivar had 8 strikes and two takedowns.

When the decision was announced, there was a fair amount of booing from the crowd. In fact, it easily drowned out any cheering. The two fighters spoke to one another. Menjivar smiled broadly, shook his head and shrugged.

In the post-fight interview, St-Pierre spoke directly to the crowd in French. He explained to the angry audience that although he had officially won the fight, Ivan had not actually intended to tap out. Instead, he had been trying to tell the ref that he was phys-ically able to keep going. That led St-Pierre to believe that, in his opinion, the fight was truly a draw.

The crowd cheered wildly. The kid from Saint Isidore stand-ing before them, still twitchy from adrenaline, had told the crowd the truth as he saw it. He didn't want anything he didn't de-serve, nothing he didn't earn. That night he set a benchmark for sportsmanship.

* * *

No matter what his own views of the bout against Menjivar were, St-Pierre officially had a 1–0 record as a professional mixed martial arts fighter. Although he may not have agreed with the decision, the people at UCC were very impressed with his performance. In fact, they thought so highly of him, they immediately gave him a shot at their welterweight title.

With a 4–1 record, Justin "Lost" Bruckmann had held the wel-terweight title since he had beaten the late Phil Hughes at *UCC 6:*

Redemption on October 19, 2001, in a grueling four-round decision. It wasn't Bruckmann's natural weight class. He actually fought best at around 155 pounds, making him a natural lightweight by the accepted mixed martial arts definition; but a lack of real competition in that class persuaded him to fight as a welterweight.

Not only was he an impressive veteran fighter, but he was also a judo master, which promised to give St-Pierre—still then known as more of a striking fighter—problems. Although St-Pierre could now call himself a professional, the prize money from one UCC match was hardly enough to live on. Although the league itself had some big-name sponsors—most notably Coors Light and LifeStyles Condoms—it didn't pay the fighters big money. Even its top competitors at the time earned no more than $15,000 a year from fighting. So St-Pierre had to train in a number of different disciplines while working at the same time. And he trained at a number of different gyms and dojos, all over Montreal.

Set for June 15, 2002 (just about a month after St-Pierre's 21st birthday), the championship match would be at an event called *UCC 10: Battle for the Belts 2002*. Interestingly, it was held in the city of Hull, Quebec (which has since been absorbed by neighboring Gatineau). This was an important move not only because Hull had its own significant English-speaking population at the time, but it was also just across the Ottawa River from the nation's capital—and Ontario, a province in which live exhibitions of mixed martial arts fighting competitions were still illegal.

Before a sold-out audience at the Robert Guertin Centre (known locally as "the Bob"), eight fights went on before the St-Pierre–Bruckmann bout. They were mostly Montreal-based fighters, and Menjivar brought his record back to 5–2 with a unanimous decision against heavily tattooed and unfortunately nicknamed American BJJ expert Jeff "The Big Frog" Curran.

From the start of their bout, their different styles were apparent. After the customary tap, the pair circled each other. Bruckmann was frenetic, dancing like a boxer. St-Pierre seemed more deliberate and tended to keep his feet more firmly planted on the ground.

To the surprise of many, it was St-Pierre who moved first with a takedown attempt, rather than trying to soften up his opponent with strikes. Just a few seconds into the match, he got his arms around Bruckmann's waist, put his left shoulder on his abdomen and took him down to the mat. St-Pierre mounted him immediately and Bruckmann had a hard time establishing any kind of guard with his legs. They moved around the canvas until Bruckmann managed to get his left leg underneath St-Pierre's right leg. He leveraged the challenger to his feet. It didn't last. Back down again, Bruckmann got his left leg behind St-Pierre's neck, but St-Pierre had no problem flicking it off. Still pushing with both legs, Bruckmann would repeatedly get St-Pierre up on his knees, but St-Pierre would fight off the move.

Then came a watershed moment. Here was St-Pierre, known as a striker, a karate guy, paired up with a judo master, a champion, a black belt holder, and he was dominating him on the ground. For anybody who thought they knew who St-Pierre was as a fighter, this fight changed their minds.

Once up and in a clinch, Bruckmann landed a hard right knee to St-Pierre's chest. He pushed Bruckmann into the ropes and dropped to his knees, which brought Bruckmann down as well. Bruckmann got back up and landed a couple of weak knees before attempting to flip St-Pierre over. It didn't happen. St-Pierre put his hands behind Bruckmann's knees. It was obvious that Bruckmann knew what was going to happen next, but there was nothing he could do about it. He went down like a sack of potatoes. It really impressed the announcers. "That wasn't even a takedown," one of them shouted into the microphone. "It was, bitch, get down."

The fight ended when St-Pierre forced Bruckmann onto his back. Bruckmann then miscalculated; he left his left arm undefended. St-Pierre seized it and set up a traditional arm bar. Bruckmann knew he was done, and he tapped out.

As soon as the ref separated them, GSP was celebrating. He ran over to his corner and was lifted and carried around the ring. In just his second fight and at just 21 years of age, St-Pierre had become a champion. There would be no apology or self-effacing speech that night.

The celebration was short-lived. St-Pierre quickly remembered his opponent. He stopped strutting and walked over to Bruckmann, who was still slowly rising from the canvas. St-Pierre made sure he was okay, then he hugged him and congratulated him on a great fight.

It went in the books as a submission via arm bar from guard at 3:23 of the first round. The statistics of the fight indicated exactly how well St-Pierre did. He landed 20 of 24 strike attempts, as opposed to Bruckmann's two of three, and two of three takedown attempts while Bruckmann failed in his only attempt.

* * *

Just two fights and less than six months into his professional mixed martial arts career, and just a month after his 21st birthday, St-Pierre was already a champion.

He learned very early, however, that no matter what you do or how well you do it, there will always be critics. There was grumbling that both men he had beaten were fighting out of their weight class and had to gain weight to fight as welterweights. Although he had clearly handled Bruckmann, even he had admitted that the verdict on the Menjivar fight was, at best, imperfect.

To silence those critics, he had to fight and beat a bigger man. The UCC's organizers found him one in Edmonton, Alberta. At 6-feet tall and with a fighting weight of 185, Travis "The Gladiator" Galbraith had two inches and 15 pounds on St-Pierre.

Although St-Pierre could reflect back on bullying at school and troubles at home, at least he had a home. Galbraith grew up far more disadvantaged. "I was in and out of trouble my whole life. I was brought up in the system. Youth detention centers were my thing. All the way until I was 18," he said. "It was just a lack of parents. They just did their own thing. For someone [who] had nothing to begin with, fighting seemed like the thing to do. I just knew I needed to apply myself to it. I was lucky that I didn't have to pay for my training in the beginning. All I had was myself."

But that didn't mean Galbraith was an unschooled or undisciplined fighter. He may have started as a street fighter, but he improved his techniques through a series of martial arts. In fact, as a professional fighting in Western Canadian mixed martial arts organizations like World Freestyle Fighting and Roadhouse Rumble, he had amassed an impressive 5–1 record with his only loss coming in a tough match against Manitoba's Joe "El Dirte" Doerksen, one of Canada's most respected middleweight fighters.

St-Pierre had already proven that he could fight professionally, and against Menjivar and Bruckmann he proved that he had the necessary ground game to compete with fighters from diverse backgrounds. It was not quite four months after he had dispatched Bruckmann that he would fight Galbraith. *UCC 11: The Next Level* was scheduled for October 11, 2002, at the Auditorium de Verdun. There would be nine fights that night—including matches featuring Doerksen, Menjivar, Bruckmann and Loiseau—but the main event would involve watching to see if St-Pierre could defend his welterweight title against a fighter who was actually a middle-weight fighting at welterweight.

Right from the start, it was a study in contrasts and in how partisan a crowd can be. The fighters looked like they came from central casting—it was the good guy against the tough guy. Galbraith wore the metaphorical black hat. When he was being in-troduced, Galbraith leaned against the ropes with a disinterested, almost bored and certainly contemptuous look on his face. When his name was announced, he twirled his upstretched index finger in the air as though he couldn't possibly care less about where he was and what was about to happen. The boos were torrential.

On the other hand, St-Pierre was a ball of energy, constantly moving. As the announcer introduced him (first in French) as undisputed champion, he jogged and shadow-boxed around the canvas to a huge chorus of cheers. After his extended introduction was finally finished, he bowed to the crowd in acknowledgment of their cheering. It was the first time the crowd had heard St-Pierre introduced as "Rush."

There have been lots of stories about how that nickname origi-nated, but many attribute it to a Patry marketing idea. It indicated that St-Pierre was in a rush to get his opponent to the ground and also played on the concept of an adrenaline rush. St-Pierre himself explained, "When I was fighting in Canada, I finished all my op-ponents in the first round, so my manager at the time thought it was very appropriate."

Although Galbraith had earlier tried to look the punk, con-temptuous of the crowd, he showed what looked like genuine respect for St-Pierre. Instead of the traditional tap to start the fight, Galbraith looked his opponent in the eyes, said something to him and shook both his hands.

Both fighters went for contact early. St-Pierre landed a light left to Galbraith's chest. Seeing his opening, Galbraith launched a hard right front kick that slammed into St-Pierre's left hip. But it left Galbraith off balance and vulnerable. St-Pierre lunged forward, planting his left shoulder into Galbraith's belly, securing his arms around his waist and lifting him off the ground. Galbraith went up about a foot and was slammed down on his back with a frightening thud.

They grappled for a while, Galbraith on the defensive the whole time, and you could hear voices calling out "Triangle! Triangle!" But there was no way St-Pierre could mount a triangle choke hold as Galbraith was protecting his throat. St-Pierre went for an arm bar. He held and stretched Galbraith's left arm and was doing his best to set him up, but the challenger wouldn't give up without a fight. St-Pierre tried to subdue him a little with a quick knee to the ribs, then managed to get his knee on top of Galbraith's arm. St-Pierre pressed his right forearm on the side of Galbraith's neck and his hand on the back of his neck. Unable to effect a choke hold, St-Pierre lifted his opponent's head off the canvas and slammed it back down again before unleashing a punch to his face.

The referee, who had been right on top of them for close to a minute, had seen enough. He called it. It was over. St-Pierre got off the prone man, stood up, slammed his fists together and shouted. Clapping his hands, he walked around the canvas before grabbing his mouth guard and throwing it up into the crowd. Then he raised his hands in the traditional champion's pose before blowing a kiss to the audience. They loved it; they were going wild.

But at least one person in the room was not celebrating. Galbraith apparently did not agree with the referee's call. He rushed at St-Pierre threateningly, before the ref slipped both of his arms under his armpits and pulled him away. St-Pierre approached the irate challenger, still held by the ref, and tried to speak with him to calm him down.

The ref and Galbraith's people did manage to calm him down, and he was sitting in his corner as St-Pierre continued to strut around the canvas, blow kisses to his fans and perform standing backflips. He ended the show by getting to his knees in the center of the ring, crossing himself and saying a prayer. He went over to shake hands and speak with Galbraith, who was by now calm but clearly unhappy.

St-Pierre won a TKO via punches at 2:03 in the first round. The stats were as one-sided as the fight appeared. GSP was credited with landing 13 of 15 strike attempts and two of two takedowns. For Galbraith, the numbers were one of one and zero for zero. There was a great deal of discussion on the Internet on the night of the fight, mostly about why Galbraith was so upset about the fight's stoppage. More than one person pointed out that no matter how long the fight lasted, there was no way in hell Galbraith was going to turn it around.

CHAPTER 4

After he dispatched Galbraith so convincingly, St-Pierre was a genuine hot commodity in Canadian mixed martial arts. He was attracting the notice of some influential people, such as Sportsnet columnist and on-air personality Joe Ferraro (also known as "Showdown Joe"), probably the best-known and most respected commentator on mixed martial arts in Canada. He later wrote:

> I remember Georges' debut and thinking to myself how impressive he was against UFC veteran Ivan Menjivar. He then proceeded to defeat one of my training partners at the time, Justin Bruckmann, to win his first title, in what was only his second pro MMA bout. After his brutal victory over Pride [Fighting Championships] veteran Travis Galbraith in his third fight, it was his fourth pro fight when it hit me: GSP was something truly special and I was witnessing something legendary unfold right before my eyes.

But St-Pierre's rising star was perhaps a little too bright. Now referred to as GSP by the media, just three months after that fight, and only seven months after the Bruckmann bout at *UCC 10*, he was scheduled to defend his belt again. *UCC 12: Adrenaline* was set for January 25, 2003, at the Centre Pierre-Charbonneau in Montreal. GSP was to fight a Californian named Thomas "The Wildman" Denny. It would be the first UCC event with a pay-per-view distributor.

Although it was just one of hundreds of mixed martial arts fights from dozens of regional organizers at the time and would not be seen by that many people, it would turn out to be one of the most important fights of GSP's career.

Although the UCC had held events in the stadium before and many of the fighters were familiar names in Montreal, there was something a little different about this event. Everything about it seemed overwrought and cartoonish, like it had the air of a WWF event rather than a mixed martial arts fight, beginning with the prefight interviews. Denny's arms were covered in tattoos and he was wearing a thick gold chain. His hair was shaved in such a way that it presented three distinct tufts sticking out—one in the middle and one on each side—and he had a W shaven onto the back of his head. His face was clean-shaven except for two more tufts of hair sprouting from each side of his chin, like a goat's beard. He went into his spiel: "Hey, I'm The Wildman, Thomas Denny. [I] came up here from California to kick some Canadian ass. And all you Canadians don't like me now, but you'll like me when I leave the ring. I'm here to fight George of the Jungle, but he better watch out for that knee." Denny does have a reputation as an eccentric and is not afraid to speak his mind, but that speech could hardly have sounded more scripted. And the whole American-Canadian rivalry thing totally smacked of the WWF, which had ridden the cross-border rivalry shtick from Day 1.

Denny's entrance into the ring further highlighted the buffoonery usually associated with professional wrestling. In the darkened auditorium, two spotlights converged on an entrance-way at the top of a long ramp. In the spotlight, Denny addressed the crowd. Surrounded by mist from a smoke machine and with loud heavy metal music blaring, he walked to the ring wearing a large skull mask with a giant parody of a horned Viking helmet on it and a robe trimmed with leopard print and plastic skulls.

The wide brush they used to paint Denny as a villain was put back to work to portray GSP as a hero. He was introduced as a "master grappler" though his reputation had been as a striker until then. He gave the same short speech in French and then English. He introduced himself as the Canadian champion and said it was his first international fight. Then he drew his fist and said, "Can you see that, Wildman? Tonight, that's for you."

He jogged down his ramp with upbeat music and was wearing an ordinary blue gi with a Japanese-style headband. He went into the ring, knelt, crossed himself and said a little prayer.

When the bell rang, each fighter came out in a boxing pose and studied the other. GSP connected first with a hard left that glanced off Denny's face, and the challenger managed to block his follow-up right while getting his own forearms behind GSP's neck. The champ got a hard right into Denny's flank, who responded with a knee that was partially blocked.

Denny was pulling hard on GSP's neck in an attempt to effect a takedown, but GSP was having none of it. He got his butt down, kept his center of gravity low and stayed on his feet. Then he went to his knees dragging a still-clasping Denny down, but not off his feet. GSP quickly got his right hand behind Denny's knee, but the tenacious challenger managed to straighten up and slip free of it.

Denny then backed his opponent up and sent a hard knee to his abdomen. They both began to look tired. By lifting and spinning him, Denny managed to get GSP's feet in the air. But it was only for a brief moment. There was more grappling, but GSP eventually managed to get free. He landed a tremendous flurry of fists before they separated again.

Denny approached, leading with his left. Seeing his best shot, GSP got low and bull-rushed Denny, bringing him to his knees. But he was back up in an instant. Just as GSP stood up with him, he twisted the action, pushing his right shoulder into Denny's chest, which put him on one foot and then on his back.

He struggled to achieve guard. As the pair searched each other for weaknesses—exchanging short punches and the occasional head butt (which were still legal in the UCC) along the way—GSP was clearly dominating. He was trying hard to get a forearm on Denny's neck, but couldn't and settled for slamming his left knee into the side of his head. Still frustrated by Denny's defenses, he kneed his head again. But that allowed Denny to get enough leverage to lift GSP onto all fours. The champ used a hard right to break Denny's push and was back on top of him. Then he began to pound his head against the canvas and land the odd right fist. The round ended with Denny on his back, unable to do anything but absorb the punishment GSP was dishing out.

GSP had certainly been in control and looked like the superior fighter. But something was seriously wrong. GSP was exhausted, so exhausted in fact that he was physically sick. Too sick, he believed, to go on. He made a hard decision. He was going to throw in the towel and forfeit the match.

It might even have been a smart strategic move. Because the UCC was a regional organization, it named GSP the *Canadian* welterweight champion. If he lost to Denny, an American citizen, he would still hold his title and belt. But, still, it would be a loss, his first; ruining an otherwise unblemished professional record. But, at the time, it seemed to make sense to GSP:

In the first round, I put him down and I beat him. I tried so hard to finish him, but the guy always managed to survive. At the end of the round, I was so tired that I could barely walk back to my corner. So I said to my cornerman: "Damn! I'm so tired; I can't go back out there." And my cornerman said, "What do you mean? You're kicking the guy's ass. Just go back out and do the same thing you're doing.'" I said, "I feel so weak; I'm going to die. I'm going to try a high kick to his head, and if that doesn't work, throw in the towel." So my cornerman looks at me and says, "Georges, I don't have any towels. Do you see any towels here?" So I think to myself, "Great, my cornerman wants me to die." I got so pissed off that my cornerman, my friend, wanted me to die in the ring. So I went back out there.

GSP did what he promised. He went out there and delivered a roundhouse kick to Denny's face. No towel entered the ring. Loiseau, his friend, was not going to let him give up. GSP had to go out there and finish Denny off, tap out or genuinely lose the fight.

GSP faked a right kick and rushed Denny. He was probably higher than he wanted to be, but his momentum and leg drive bowled Denny over and onto his back. GSP then switched from the front to a side mount. Denny was back in the same position that he was for much of the first round—on his back and struggling to find anything that would free him.

GSP managed to break Denny's guard. He got into a perfect position, sitting on Denny's belly and pounding him in the head with his fists. Denny managed to get his arms locked around GSP's waist and bring him down far enough to stop the barrage of fists.

GSP then broke his grip and started punching again, but Denny managed to roll to his right, knocking GSP off his mount.

By this time, most of Denny's face was battered, and he was bleeding badly from the nose. With GSP back on top of him, Denny tried a few weak punches to the back of the champ's head, which, like head butting, was still legal in the UCC.

In a clinch, both fighters looked tired. Denny managed a hard knee to GSP's abdomen. GSP answered in kind. While Denny was up against the ropes, trying to figure out how to land a blow, GSP managed to drag him back down. GSP was on top, but Denny had an effective guard so there was little either fighter could do but exchange weak punches.

Back up on their knees and then on their feet, they clinched—interrupted only by knees to the body—until GSP brought Denny back down again. From side mount, a clearly rejuvenated GSP slammed Denny's head to the canvas, then threw in a pair of hard knees and punches.

The ref jumped in and separated the pair. It was over. GSP—who only a few minutes earlier was going to forfeit—had won convincingly.

His celebration—which took place while Denny's cornerman used towels to stop his nose from bleeding—was more subdued than previous ones. He mounted the turnbuckle for a gun show, then demonstrated some break dancing moves in the middle of the ring. The two fighters met and had what seemed like a friendly exchange, then GSP grabbed a towel and tied it on his head much like the headband he had on before the fight. As the announcer named GSP the winner, Denny applauded him and the pair exchanged a brief hug. Then, clearly no longer exhausted, GSP went back into his gymnastics and break-dancing routine.

Officially, the fight ended at 4:45 of the second round as a TKO because of cuts Denny suffered. GSP was awarded twenty-five landed strikes to Denny's seven and five takedowns to Denny's zero.

Joe Ferraro, who was already aware of and impressed by GSP, considered the fight to be an epiphany:

> When GSP was originally matched up against Thomas "The Wildman" Denny, I vividly recall voting down this matchup as I thought Georges was overmatched. Denny was 10–9 and had fought some big names coming into this bout. He had quite the name for himself, and I just felt Georges wasn't ready for such a big challenge so early on in his career. How wrong I was. Georges proceeded to dismantle Denny and crush the veteran en route to a TKO victory in the second round. The turning point for me was GSP's double leg entry in the first round as well as all of his takedowns and ground control. I thought to myself: "This guy is on another level." He was simply too much for a fighter I had high regard for. It was like Georges was the veteran and Denny was the younger fighter. It not only opened my eyes to how good GSP was but it was a defining moment in my own MMA career as I was watching the birth of a legend less than five feet from where I was sitting.

The Denny fight was a watershed moment for GSP, in which just about every sports cliché about believing in yourself, playing through pain and never giving up can be applied. The Bruckmann fight may have given him the title, but it was the Denny fight that proved he was a champion.

* * *

Clearly, GSP was the best fighter Patry had in his stable. Everybody wanted a piece of him. And the times were changing. Mixed martial arts was gaining popularity throughout North America. By the middle of 2003, the UFC—reorganized and reinvigorated after the change in ownership—had established itself as the premier professional mixed martial arts organization, with events that had no problem filling 10,000-seat arenas, and was getting pay-per-view buy rates approaching six digits again.

After it had started attracting a few American viewers and quality American fighters like Denny, the UCC caught the attention of the UFC. The two organizations established a working agreement under one condition—the UCC had to change its name, which sounded too much like UFC. So in the spring of 2003, the UCC morphed into a new company called the TKO Major League MMA.

The organization's next big fight after *UCC 12* (there was a *UCC Proving Ground 9* at a hotel in Victoriaville, about two hours' drive east of Montreal) was called *TKO 13: Ultimate Rush*. The name was misleading. Back at the Centre Pierre-Charbonneau, *TKO 13* featured 13 fights with some well-known Québécois fighters, a few from Ontario and British Columbia and one from Arizona, but there was no GSP. In effect, there was no "Rush" in the *Ultimate Rush*.

There was supposed to be. In fact, GSP was scheduled to fight an opponent who had a much better résumé than any fighter he had ever faced before. Pete "The Secret Weapon" Spratt was originally from north Texas and had a 12–6 record with six submissions, three KOs and two TKOs as a professional. Known as a major striker—he trained primarily in muay Thai—he also had begun to develop grappling techniques. Most notably, Spratt had already had three fights in the UFC—forcing Robbie "Ruthless" Lawler and Zach "The Lisbon Outlaw" Light to submit, and losing a close one when Carlos "The Ronin" Newton caught him with an arm bar. Lawler was 9–0 when he met Spratt at *UFC 42: Sudden Impact* in Miami and Spratt dominated him completely and put him out of commission for quite a while.

That fight put Spratt into title contention. His star was rising, but he did something that angered the powers at the UFC—he turned down the chance at a title fight. He knew he needed to do something to get back into their good graces. "I was on the shelf for a brief moment with the UFC at that particular time because I believe that was around the time I turned down the title fight with Matt Hughes," he said. "So the UFC put me on the back burner and I needed to work. My manager called me about fighting for TKO and I was just looking for a good opportunity, and at the time TKO was a very reputable organization."

But it didn't happen—at least not at that time. Unwilling to fight again when he was not in top condition—and wary after his experiences with Denny—GSP backed out of the fight. It was not a popular move. Mixed martial arts forums on the Internet exploded with disdain for GSP. "Originally I was scheduled to fight GSP at *TKO 13* and he pulled out the day before the fight due to an infection in his knee, I believe," Spratt said. "I was really pissed off about that because they knew well in advance that he was hurt and flew me all the way out there for nothing."

But Spratt didn't have to wait long to meet GSP. The big match was rescheduled for TKO's next event. The Colisée des Bois-Francs in downtown Victoriaville was chosen to host *TKO 14: Road Warriors*. It was set for November 29, 2003—more than 10 months after GSP's fight with Denny, and almost three months after he postponed his bout with Spratt.

The fight got in the way of Spratt's career advancement. "So we ended up having to reschedule for November at *TKO 14*," he told me. "During that time the UFC called me to fight Karo Parisyan, but I was under contractual obligations to face GSP."

In fact, when the UFC announced the card for *UFC 46: Supernatural*, to be held in Las Vegas the following January, Spratt was back in their good books and scheduled to fight Parisyan, a rising star with a 10–2 record as a professional. It would not be a title fight, but could well have led to one. Spratt's scheduled fight against GSP, on the other hand, was in what many mixed martial arts observers considered a minor-league organization, and was viewed by many as nothing more than a warm-up bout. Spratt, however, took it very seriously. "I really didn't know anything about Georges. I knew he was an undefeated fighter, and it was going to be a great test for me as with any undefeated fighter," he said. "I am always up to take on challenges, and it always seems like I am going to hostile territory; but this is the profession I chose, so I had to take these opportunities."

In the prefight interview, Spratt was confident and conversational. He described himself as "a pretty aggressive fighter," and said, "Unfortunately, he's the guy in front of me who's going to have to take my wrath. And he's going to get knocked out." While Denny had been quite blatantly portrayed as a villain before his fight with GSP, Spratt came off as a likeable, intelligent young man, certainly not a bad guy. But the organizers couldn't help pointing out that he was an American fighting a Canadian on Canadian soil. In a seemingly scripted prefight speech—it's hard to tell actually, as Spratt is a talented part-time actor as well as a fighter—he said that he'd rather be with his family on "this holiday weekend," a reference to American Thanksgiving. He also mentioned that he wanted to "finish some unfinished business"—a reference to their postponed match.

In his own interview, GSP pointed out that none of his fights had gone to the limit and promised that this one wouldn't either. Referring to comments Spratt made to a blogger about being disappointed that GSP backed out of *TKO 13*, the Canadian champ said: "I'm happy that he doesn't respect me on the Internet. He is giving me more anger and hate to train harder. When I catch this guy, he won't be able to understand anything [a Québécois expression analogous to 'I'll knock the sense out of him']. I want to go for a TKO or submission."

Spratt was introduced first. He had a boxing-style robe prominently sponsored by Tapout, a burgeoning fight apparel company. GSP came in later. He strode to the ring to the musical stylings of the Wu-Tang Clan, wearing a blue gi adorned with the logos of a few small-time sponsors and his now familiar headband. The partisan announcers introduced GSP as the "darling of Saint Isidore" and pointed out that he was "dangerous" on the ground and "a specialist in submissions."

When they took their robes off, the audience could see another sponsor's logo. Both fighters had the name GoldenPalace. com temporarily tattooed on their backs in huge letters. GoldenPalace.com already had a history of putting its name on fighters (and other attention-getters like streakers and free climbers) by that point. "Yeah, the henna tattoos were all about extra money for us," Spratt said. "They were getting really big in boxing at the time, and we got the opportunity to make a little extra for wearing them during our fight." And it was an interesting—if not perhaps dubious—choice of sponsors for an event striving to become a mainstream, respectable sport since GoldenPalace. com is a gambling website owned by the Kahnawake Mohawks.

Despite some harsh words before the fight, the opponents greeted each other in a friendly and respectful manner.

At the start, both fighters kept their distance. That was a good idea on both fighters' parts. Spratt had a devastating leg kick that could KO an opponent with one blow. In fact, many years later, GSP would answer "Pete Spratt" when he was asked which of his opponents had the most powerful striking ability. And GSP had acquired ground fighting skills that could quickly put Spratt in serious trouble.

GSP made the first foray with a low left roundhouse kick that grazed Spratt. He followed that with a couple of quick jabs that didn't come close. He was still retreating from that when Spratt launched a powerful right roundhouse that GSP had to jump to avoid. Spratt tried to follow it up with a quick high left kick, but GSP ducked it and went in for the takedown. "I wouldn't say my strategy was to come out kicking, but I definitely wanted him to taste my kicking power. Kicking is not something you want to do first thing in a fight when all the other person wants to do is take you down," Spratt recalled. "When you watch our fight, I threw a push kick and he shot straight away for the takedown. That was an early and fateful mistake for me in that fight."

Indeed. While Spratt's left foot was still in the air, GSP grabbed it and managed to spin Spratt onto his back. It was clear that GSP was in his element as Spratt was struggling to get up while GSP slowly and patiently searched for openings. Unable to find any, GSP delivered a few quick punches to Spratt's head. The two grappled and exchanged punches with GSP in mount. He achieved a side mount, but was unable to finish off his opponent.

As Spratt—who is not known for his ground game—fought with some effectiveness against the side mount, he was unprepared for when GSP switched to a full mount. Spratt used his remarkable leg strength to pop GSP up onto all fours. Still underneath, Spratt managed to turn over and get to his hands and feet, carrying

GSP on his back, piggyback style. But it was not a good position for Spratt. He went back down, GSP riding him and delivering punches.

As they twisted, Spratt managed to break GSP's hold and leapt on top of him. Immediately, GSP hooked his legs around Spratt and the two were back to punching each other. Then, with a giant leg kick, GSP turned the tables by spinning the pair of them to put Spratt on his back. The crowd screamed its approval.

With Spratt's arms locked around his chest, GSP managed to lift him up and slam him to the mat. But Spratt spun onto his belly for a better defensive position.

He made a strategic decision. He was going to use his powerful legs to get back up to standing with GSP still on his back. Although he managed that remarkable feat, it backfired on him. With his hands busy trying to protect his throat, Spratt inadvertently allowed GSP to get him in a rear-naked choke.

The pair fell over backward, with all of Spratt's weight falling onto GSP. But he did not let go. The choke held. Spratt tapped and, with 1:12 left in the first round, it was over.

GSP ran out from underneath the still-reeling Spratt and did a standing front flip in the middle of the ring. The crowd was deafening. After blowing kisses to the audience, GSP walked over to the still-sitting Spratt and said something in his ear. "It was something to the effect that I was an idol of his and he respected me," Spratt said. "I don't remember exactly, but I do remember he was very appreciative of having the opportunity to fight me."

As was now becoming familiar to his fans, GSP went into his break dancing routine and put on a show, pounding his chest for the crowd. They loved it.

The fight represented yet another profound event in GSP's young career. By beating Spratt—a bona fide UFC contender—he opened up the eyes of the mixed martial arts world. Little known outside Quebec until then, GSP's decisive victory over Spratt sent shockwaves through the industry and forced the powers that were to recognize that this undefeated fighter from *la belle province* was something more than a regional phenomenon. In fact, it made it impossible for the greater mixed martial arts community to ignore his presence any longer.

And it also helped define him as a person. In a move that would be unheard of in either boxing or wrestling, GSP decided to take Spratt out on the town after the fight. "GSP and I hung out after the fight, and he showed me a great time out there. I really enjoyed myself," Spratt recalled. "Victoriaville was great, just a bit cold for me."

CHAPTER

GSP's victory over Pete Spratt didn't just send shockwaves through the mixed martial arts world; it vaulted him into the big time.

Game changer or not, he was far from the polished, ready-for-prime-time celebrity he is now. An interview with MMARingReport.com, a small-town Pennsylvania-based online magazine, shows a representation of what he was like back then. The interview took place immediately after the Spratt fight (and, presumably, before the pair hit the bright lights of Victoriaville that evening). GSP didn't yet know he was going to fight in the UFC, but he knew bigger and better things were coming.

His trademark grin is there, but his face lacks the studied calmness it has now. Instead, he was twitchy, perhaps full of post-fight adrenaline. He had acne on his forehead and chewed pink bubblegum throughout the interview, even blowing a few bubbles. His English is improved, but it's obvious he isn't confident with his ability to use the language yet. Like many people who aren't used to being recorded, he tended to lean in too close to the microphone.

When describing the fight, he referred to his "ape technique." Inspired, he said, by how Matt Hughes beat Frank Trigg with a similarly applied rear-naked choke, GSP claimed that it was this "ape technique" that beat Spratt. He acknowledged Spratt's striking ability and said that he "played it smart" by trying to get Spratt on the mat as early as he could. "The smartest fighter [won] tonight," he said. Even now, years later, people still jokingly use the "ape technique" phrase to either criticize or praise GSP.

Then the interviewer pointed out that although Spratt was scheduled to fight Karo "The Heat" Parisyan at *UFC 46: Supernatural* in Las Vegas on January 31, 2004, GSP might be a more deserving opponent for the tough Armenian, who had just convincingly won his first fight in the UFC, defeating veteran Dave Strasser. GSP replied: "For sure, I want to go fight in [the] UFC, but I want to wish [Spratt] good luck for his fight. But, like you asked me, my dream is to go fight in [the] UFC; you know, since I [was] young. I saw Royce Gracie when I was young. When I saw this guy kick people's ass when he was smaller than everybody. I dream to go there once. Once or a couple of times to make my name over there."

His UFC dream came true. The UFC dropped Spratt from the *UFC 46* lineup and replaced him with GSP. It might have been a controversial move, but it was also a pragmatic one. Once GSP proved himself against Spratt, there was no denying that he was a hot property. He wasn't just undefeated, he was dominating. And he was marketable, handsome and a showman, but with a small-town—almost aw, shucks—innocence and lack of pretense that made him a can't-miss prospect

Held at the Mandalay Bay Resort and Casino complex in Las Vegas, GSP's UFC debut certainly looked big-time. The Octagon was full of big-time sponsors' names and logos. The production values both live and on video were worlds away from what TKO was capable of.

The event started slowly. The first bout on the preliminary card featured future welterweight champion and future GSP rival Matt "The Terror" Serra against Jeff "The Big Frog" Curran, who had lost to GSP's friend Ivan Menjivar back in 2002 at *UCC 10*. After three grueling rounds, the judges unanimously named Serra the victor of all three rounds, 30–27. He was clearly the superior fighter in the match—especially when the action was on the mat—but he was hardly dominant.

That bout was followed by American rising star Josh "The Punk" Thomson facing undefeated Brazilian Hermes "The Unreal" França in a lightweight match. It didn't lack hype. After França guaranteed he'd win in a prefight interview, Thomson mocked him by entering the ring with a *luchador* mask, like Mexican wrestlers wear. But it was even less decisive than the Serra-Curran bout. Both fighters thought they had won the match, but the judges unanimously gave it to Thomson, 29–28.

Then it was time for the GSP-Parisyan fight. Both fighters were the same height and GSP weighed in at 167, two pounds less than his rival. The announcers referred to Parisyan as "the Armenian with the bad, bad attitude." Born in Yerevan, the capital of Armenia, when that country was still part of the Soviet Union, Parisyan's family immigrated to the Armenian enclave in North Hollywood, California, when he was six. He took up judo when he was nine, and was generally regarded as the most successful mixed martial arts fighter ever to come from a traditional judo, rather than Brazilian jiu-jitsu, background.

Announcer Joe Rogan said that GSP was "absolutely overwhelmed and thrilled to have a chance to fight here in the States in his first international bout" and that "he comes with a big reputation in Canada . . . very well known up there . . . big champion in the TKO, the former UCC, and supposed to be a freakishly strong guy."

GSP wore bright white trunks that, unlike Parisyan's, carried no sponsor's brand. Although Parisyan came from a solid judo and grappling background, both fighters came out kicking. At one point in Round One, it looked like it was over. On top of GSP, Parisyan began to extend GSP's right arm, setting up a classic kimura. Not only an incredibly effective move derived from judo that causes extreme pain by twisting an opponent's arm, it's also how Parisyan dispatched Strasser so convincingly in his previous UFC bout.

But GSP began to take control with the "ground-and-pound." The move consists of GSP getting on top of his opponent (who has guard) on the ground-and-pound him with strikes until he either submits or makes a mistake that will allow GSP to apply a killer choke or lock. Parisyan did take advantage of a left hook that flew wide and almost achieved a triangle choke hold, but GSP slipped it off quickly. GSP landed punch after punch and elbow after elbow while preventing his opponent from doing anything effective, with Parisyan unsuccessfully trying to establish chokes, arm locks and leg locks. It stayed that way until the horn sounded to end the round.

It was a very confident GSP who came out for the second round. Almost as soon as it began, he landed a powerful left to Parisyan's face. When Parisyan attempted to reply in kind, GSP charged at his thighs and put him down on the canvas.

With 2:20 left in the second round, GSP opened up a cut just above Parisyan's right eye. GSP continued to hammer him with punches and elbows. It was a potentially dangerous strategy because each strike briefly opened up his body to a potential attack from below. But after the blood started flowing, Parisyan's confidence seemed to drain. He threw fewer strikes and lock attempts after that, instead keeping his hands in to defend his face. Rogan, the respected UFC analyst who had been firmly in Parisyan's corner throughout the match, said that Parisyan looked calm and relaxed. The round ended with a bloodied Parisyan on his back, shoved up against the fence with GSP on top of him, hammering away.

The third round opened with GSP again looking very confident and Parisyan appearing cautious. GSP initiated the action with a left high kick that Parisyan blocked, then followed it up with a Superman punch that sent Parisyan flying backward. He quickly recovered and threw a right punch, but it didn't come close to connecting.

GSP followed that with a left kick that made a loud thud when it hit Parisyan's thigh. Designed to affect Parisyan's mobility, the kick left GSP off balance and he began to stumble backward, but Parisyan could not take advantage; he could not move quickly enough. Then GSP saw an opening and lunged at Parisyan's knees. Parisyan was ready for it and twisted so that the takedown he knew he couldn't stop would bring him to his knees, not his back. Significantly, he held and took control of GSP's right arm. Parisyan had been showing a desire to achieve a kimura all night, and looked like he was going to try that route again.

From the position he was in, the next moves to setting up a classic kimura were fundamental—get up, flip your opponent to the ground and twist. It's basic, but it's not easy—especially against such a strong opponent. Parisyan did manage to get to his feet, but he failed to take GSP down. Back on the mat with GSP on top again, Parisyan maintained his lock on GSP's right arm. He tried another basic and proven move that he had used against Strasser.

He put his right leg between GSP's legs in an attempt at a sweep—a move that would take GSP's foot from under him and send him to the ground using the leverage of a body roll.

He succeeded. He flipped GSP onto his back and kept hold of his arm. It looked like it was going to be over. The fight that was so thoroughly one-sided in GSP's favor looked like it was going to end in a quick submission for Parisyan. He extended the arm, going in for the kill, when somehow GSP managed to roll them both over. In the blink of an eye, Parisyan found himself going from just about to gain a submission to back on his back absorbing a fresh set of hard blows from GSP.

That ground-and-pound went on for more than a full minute before the ref stopped them, as is within his purview, and told them "let's stand up." With 90 seconds left in the final round, GSP landed a huge right high kick. Parisyan launched a half-hearted takedown attempt with his head and shoulders that GSP pushed off and paid back with a strong uppercut. GSP made a couple more kick attempts, then Parisyan went into a bull rush. Again, GSP pushed him off.

Just as it looked like Parisyan was diving in again, GSP grabbed his head and delivered a jumping high knee that landed on Parisyan's chest. Then he went for a takedown and Parisyan landed in a sitting position, but managed to get up quickly. Then it happened again. With just a few seconds left, Parisyan went back to what was beginning to seem like his only trick and grabbed GSP's right arm. The horn blew. GSP jumped from on top of Parisyan and began celebrating with a series of backflips. As the judges' decision was announced, GSP waggled his tongue at the camera and made a shout-out to Canada.

It was a unanimous decision, with Abe Belardo and Glenn Trowbridge scoring it 30–27 and Nelson Hamilton giving Parisyan more credit with a 29–28 score. The stats—which are a bit skewed because of the fighters' styles—were even more one-sided, as GSP landed an incredible 138 of 177 strikes (Parisyan hit on 23 of 33) and was 6 of 8 on takedowns, and Parisyan had none.

*   *   *

With his victory over Parisyan, GSP had made the big time. At just 22 years old, he had a 1–0 record in the only universally recognized international mixed martial arts league and a perfect 6–0 record as a professional. But being big-time did not mean big money. Although *UFC 46* had filled 10,700 seats at the massive Mandalay Bay Events Center, for a reported gate of $1.377 million, and sold in excess of 80,000 pay-per-view subscriptions, it was not a huge payday for GSP. He was paid $3,000 for fighting and another $3,000 for winning.

Although $6,000 was nothing more than chump change when one considers how much training went into the 15 minutes of fighting and how brutal and grueling those 15 minutes were, it should also be noted that it was just his initiation to the league, almost an internship. The big winners that night—besides the UFC itself, of course—were the two fighters who decided the UFC's light heavyweight championship. Brazilian Vitor "The Phenom" Belfort earned $100,000 for fighting and another $30,000 for winning. His opponent, the much better known and heavily favored Randy "The Natural" Couture, took home $120,000 for participating and would have pocketed another $80,000 had he won. Not a bad payoff for 49 seconds of work. And besides, the better known guys had sponsors.

After beating Spratt, GSP told a reporter that he wanted to go to the UFC "once or a couple of times to make my name there." And he'd get a chance for a second fight less than five months later.

UFC 48: Payback was set for June 19, 2004, at the same Mandalay Bay arena that housed *UFC 46* and numerous other UFC events. The title referred to a non-championship heavyweight bout between Kimo Leopoldo, a taekwondo master who had come close to beating Royce Gracie at *UFC 3: The American Dream*, and Ken Shamrock, who had lost to Royce Gracie at *UFC 1*, but fought him to a draw at *UFC 5: The Return of the Beast* and had beaten Leopoldo at *UFC 8: David vs. Goliath*.

GSP's fight would again be on the preliminary card, where he would be joined by his old friend Ivan Menjivar, who would be making his own UFC debut against rising American star Matt "The Terror" Serra in a lightweight bout.

GSP would be facing another promising young fighter. After being adopted by the Hieronymous family, Jay "The Thoroughbred" Hieron (he shortened the name because he was tired of people pronouncing it "hairy mouse") grew up in Freeport, New York. It's a community on Long Island that has a very pleasant south side and a quite rough north side. "I didn't grow up in the best area and I was getting chased home every day. I'd run to the 7-Eleven and call my sisters who were older to come pick me up," he said. "They still make fun of me about that. They're always teasing me about how I'm a pro fighter and I used to call them every day to come save my ass."

Though just 91 pounds, he joined the Freeport High School wrestling team as a freshman looking for a way to defend himself and showed enormous early talent. After high school he went to a junior college in Iowa because it would have allowed him an easier entry to the greatly respected University of Iowa wrestling team, but he left after a few weeks because of the "culture shock" he endured by going from Long Island to an endless landscape of cornfields.

Back on Long Island, he led his Nassau Community College team to the national junior college wrestling championship. That led to a move four miles down the Meadowbrook State Parkway to Hofstra University. Although he did well in his classes and was a star on the wrestling team, it wasn't a great time for him. "Even though wrestling was going well for me, I was getting into problems in the off-season. I was getting into shit whenever wrestling didn't occupy my time," he said. "I was hanging out in the streets all night on Pearsall Avenue back in Freeport. Getting into fights, smoking weed, just basically up to no good." Even though he had been warned about drug tests before the season began, he tested positive as a senior and was kicked off the team.

Although he still had his scholarship and was not far from graduation, Hieron quit school but didn't quit his involvement with drugs. After some associates ratted on him, he went to jail until his family bailed him out. With the help of a good lawyer and many letters from coaches and others backing up his character, Hieron avoided any prison time, instead getting five years' probation.

Eventually he turned it all around. Initially getting into boxing to work off his aggression and stress, he became involved in mixed martial arts at the urging of some workout pals. He stayed out of trouble and had amassed a 4–0 record as a professional before making his UFC debut against GSP at *UFC 48*.

A worthy opponent Hieron may have been, he wasn't the UFC's first choice for this fight. Instead, the officials had selected another welterweight, Jason "Mayhem" Miller. A certified eccentric who made Thomas Denny appear subtle in comparison, Miller was an accomplished fighter who had an impressive 11–3 record for a variety of mixed martial arts organizations and was scheduled to make his UFC debut against GSP. But he would have to wait. Miller spent much of 2004 in and out of courtrooms as he fought charges stemming from an October 2003 fight in Atlanta in which he allegedly broke another man's nose. He eventually pled guilty to aggravated battery and received five years' probation in November 2004, but the UFC wanted no part of him while the trial was active.

The fight itself came with little fanfare as it was part of the preliminary matches. Most people were there to see Shamrock and Leopoldo or the heavyweight championship bout that pitted Frank Mir against Tim "The Maine-iac" Sylvia.

Hieron wore black boxing-style trunks with a picture of a horse reflecting his nickname "Thoroughbred," while GSP wore his now-familiar tight white trunks. Notably, neither had a sponsor. But there was one big change compared to what viewers saw at *UFC 46*. The announcers, including Rogan, no longer spoke about how GSP was happy just to be there. They were treating him like the veteran, or at least the favorite to win.

Hieron struck first, a little left kick to GSP's thigh. GSP followed that up with a quick left to the face. After it worked, he threw a couple more. These weren't big punches; they had an exploratory feel to them. Then Hieron threw a punch that GSP ducked. Seeing an opening, GSP went for Hieron's midsection, but Hieron managed to gain separation before GSP could set up a proper takedown.

As had been his strategy in his last few fights, GSP had been concentrating on his ground-and-pound. It wasn't pretty, but it was plenty effective. But what happened next came from his roots as a kyokushin karate expert and his more recent boxing training. With just less than four minutes to go in the first round, GSP unleashed a wicked right that caught Hieron square in the jaw. Hieron's eyes rolled back in his head and he went down like a sack of potatoes. The crowd screamed its approval.

Hitting the ground knocked Hieron back into consciousness and he lunged to grab GSP's knees. They got up to their feet in a clinch and quickly separated. GSP threw a couple of big lefts and a right. Hieron was reeling, listing strongly to his right. After righting himself, Hieron started to retreat as GSP lunged in with more punches. Hieron ran out of room. When he hit the fence, he went down again. GSP gained position on top of him and, while still on his feet and then on his knees, pelted the supine Hieron with a terrifying number of punches and elbows. With 3:19 left, referee Steve Mazzagatti yelled "Stop! Stop!"

It was over. GSP got off his vanquished opponent and went to the center of the ring for his familiar celebration. But he didn't land his backflip properly, landing on his knees. That prompted Rogan to say, "He might've hurt himself more with that flip than the whole fight." Recovered, GSP went into his signature break dance routine.

After his bout with Spratt, GSP mentioned that he took pride in being a smart fighter. In that match, he was careful to avoid and then later neutralize Spratt's primary weapon—his powerful leg kicks. And in this fight, he prevented a wrestler from getting comfortable by staying off the ground and pummeling him with his fists. Not only was GSP proving to be a smart fighter, he had shown the amazing ability to adopt starkly contrasting styles in response to his opponents' strengths and weaknesses. It was reminiscent of Bruce Lee, who won success by combining traditional styles and adapting within the fight. As an open-minded student of many disciplines, coaches and masters, GSP was able to do the same thing.

The stats on the fight hardly tell the complete story. GSP landed 23 of 32 strike attempts while Hieron hit on just 3 of 7. Neither man had a successful takedown (GSP had just one attempt, Hieron three). FightMetric, a statistics and analysis firm that is the official scorer of UFC fights, gave GSP a performance rating of 97 out of 100 and Hieron a 5.

It was scored as a standing TKO at 1:45 of the first round, and it left GSP with a 7–0 record as a professional fighter and 2–0 in the UFC.

And his payday improved as well. The event had a little trouble attracting live fans—they filled all the seats, but only 6,528 in attendance actually paid for tickets, the rest were comped. But with a $901,655 gate, the UFC sold a very respectable 110,000 pay-per-view subscriptions. While almost 30 percent of the total fighter payout went to just 1 of the 16 fighters (Shamrock, who beat Leopoldo with a first round TKO and earned $170,000), GSP saw a significant raise to $8,000 ($4,000 for fighting and another $4,000 for winning).

*   *   *

While GSP had proven himself a legitimate UFC fighter, he was hardly the hottest property—or the most-talked-about fighter—in his weight class at the time. As he was beginning to establish himself as a fighter, the welterweight class was ruled by a soft-spoken young born-again Christian from the Midwest named Matt Hughes. He'd made his UFC debut at *UFC 22: There Can Only Be One Champion* on September 24, 1999, after compiling an impressive 8–1 record for other organizations and convincingly beating respected Bulgarian Valeri Ignatov.

Hughes kept fighting for various organizations and had compiled a 29–3 record as a professional (2–1 in the UFC) when he was offered a shot at the welterweight title at *UFC 34: High Voltage* on November 2, 2001. The belt holder at the time was Canadian Carlos "The Ronin" Newton. Born on the Caribbean island of Anguilla, Newton grew up in Newmarket, just north of Toronto and began learning Brazilian jiu-jitsu as a young man with a dojo in Toronto. Few considered him a truly top-flight fighter, even after he managed to wrest the welterweight title away from Pat "The Croatian Sensation" Miletich at *UFC 31: Locked & Loaded* six months earlier with a bulldog choke.

The fight against Hughes was Newton's first title defense and it did not go well. With just 87 seconds gone in the first round, Hughes scored a TKO with a huge body slam. After that, Hughes saw lots of fights but very little competition in his class. While GSP was working his way up through UCC/TKO and in his beginning stages of UFC competition, Hughes defended his title five times in less than a year and a half, defeating Hayato "Mach" Sakurai, Newton in a rematch, Gil Castillo, Sean "The Muscle Shark" Sherk and Frank "Twinkle Toes" Trigg. Only Sherk, a very big name in his own right, managed to take him the distance.

Hughes wasn't just winning, he was dominating. People seemed to relate to him. "I'm not in love with the idea of being in the spotlight," he said. "It's nice and it is an ego stroke, but I read the Bible every day to keep myself grounded. Other fighters might live for the attention, but I don't. One day I am going to wash my hands of the sport and walk away. I want to make my money while I can. I want to make my money and then go home and raise my family on my farm." He was a successful ambassador for the sport and he won over many fans. One of those fans, by his own admission, was GSP himself.

But while there didn't appear to be a welterweight fighter who could dethrone Hughes, there was one fighter many thought could challenge him. His name was BJ "The Prodigy" Penn. Originally from Hawaii, Penn trained with the Gracies in Brazil and in 2000 became the first non-Brazilian to win the Brazilian jiu-jitsu world championship. With a 5–1–1 professional record, Penn was the reigning lightweight champion.

With no viable challengers for him in the lightweight class, and Hughes facing a similar situation in the welterweight division, Penn decided to move up a weight class and challenge Hughes. The fight was set up for the same *UFC 46* event in which GSP made his UFC debut. Hughes was heavily favored.

Penn had done an outstanding job of bulking up and, if anything, looked even larger than Hughes. Right from the beginning, Penn appeared to be in control, getting Hughes where he wanted him—on the mat—very quickly. Though decidedly in Penn's element, Hughes fought back gamely and made a fight out of it, especially when it came to standing and striking. But it was a quick punch from Penn that decided the match. With it, Penn started Hughes's nose bleeding. Without thinking, Hughes made a fatal mistake. Protecting his nose from Penn, he turned away from him. Penn wasted no time getting behind Hughes and applying a rear-naked choke. Just before the end of the first round, Hughes tapped out.

Penn was now the UFC's lightweight *and* welterweight champion. But he then made a move that he later described as a mistake that stemmed from immaturity and a lack of proper perspective. Citing a lack of realistic challengers in the UFC, Penn signed a contract with K-1, a rival mixed martial arts organization based in Tokyo.

Immediately, the UFC stripped Penn of the welterweight title, pointing out a clause in his contract that required him to defend any title he held at least once or forfeit it. Penn then launched a lawsuit against Zuffa, the UFC's parent company, claiming they had breached that contract. He wanted his title back, cash damages and received an injunction that prevented the UFC from naming a welterweight champion while the case was pending.

So from around the time GSP made his UFC debut in January 2004 until the autumn of that year, the UFC had no welterweight champion. But on September 29, 2004, Clark County (Nevada) District Court Judge Ken Cory struck down Penn's injunction, allowing the UFC to name a new welterweight champion.

There was speculation at the time among fans and media that the UFC would just give the title back to Hughes, but they made him fight for it. The erstwhile champion would have to win the belt back by fighting the best welterweight challenger the UFC could find. So at *UFC 50: The War of '04,* set for October 22, 2004, at the Trump Plaza in Atlantic City, New Jersey, the 36–4 Hughes had to fight the only welterweight left with a chance at beating him. It was the new kid, the undefeated phenom, Georges St-Pierre.

CHAPTER 6

The mixed martial arts world was alive with excitement before *UFC 50*. Everyone was concentrating on whether the chastened good ol' boy former champ could reclaim his belt, or if it would go to the young French-Canadian upstart who had looked so unbeatable in his first few fights.

Although the myth of Matt Hughes's invincibility had been shattered by BJ Penn's rear-naked choke nine months earlier, he was still a fighter who had won 13 straight matches before that and successfully defended his championship five times. He was enormously strong, specializing in lifting his opponents off their feet and slamming them to the canvas. Beating him would be a formidable task for anyone.

GSP was very athletic and had shown remarkable discipline, patience and resourcefulness for someone his age. And in many critics' eyes, his age and overall lack of experience were his only weaknesses. Consensus reached by observers in the mixed martial arts world—one that was articulated by Hughes himself before the fight—was that although GSP would without a doubt be a champion one day, facing a future hall-of-famer like Hughes at or near the peak of his career would be just too big a challenge for such a young man. His day would come, conventional wisdom dictated, but not against Hughes. At least not at *UFC 50*.

A more pragmatic and less competitive fighter than GSP probably would have considered himself to be in the cat-bird seat, in a nothing-to-lose situation. If he were to win the fight, he'd be champion, and if he were to lose, his reputation would still be intact because it just wasn't his time.

For his part, GSP made a show of confidence: "For me it's a win, an achievement—the huge achievement of my life. I ain't scared. I control my fear, and I ain't scared of Matt Hughes," he said. "Everybody's going to be very surprised. I will shock the world."

GSP made his entrance in his signature white headband and a blue gi covered in sponsorship patches. He strode confidently, high-fiving the odd fan along the way (one fan unfurled a Mohawk warriors flag for the cameras as GSP passed by) as the arena was filled with a sonic bombardment of Kanye West's hip-hop song "Jesus Walks."

In a direct contrast to GSP's athletic and bass-fueled jog up to the Octagon, Hughes—wearing a plain white T-shirt and boxing trunks—walked slowly down the path accompanied (as always) by Hank Williams Jr.'s somber and twangy 1982 song "A Country Boy Can Survive." He barely looked up and did not do much to acknowledge the crowd.

Play-by-play man Mike Goldberg and commentator Frank Mir (the reigning UFC heavyweight champ was filling in for color analyst Joe Rogan who was touring with his comedy act) discussed how incredibly strong Hughes was. Goldberg pointed out that 280-pound heavyweight Tim Sylvia had once jumped on 170-pound Hughes's back, and Hughes had stood up and carried Sylvia to a corner and "sat him back down." Mir agreed that kind of thing was easily possible for Hughes and pointed out his strength could be overwhelming in the upcoming bout. "If he gets his hands around St-Pierre, St-Pierre is going to be taken down," he said. "There's no choice in the matter."

When he was introduced, GSP received a mix of cheers and boos, and he repaid his detractors with a smirk and his fans with a bow. The cheers for Hughes were absolutely torrential. He acknowledged them with a modest wave. GSP looked, as usual, fit and strong, but Hughes was incredibly thick with muscle, looking like a cartoon caricature of a muscleman or a bulldog.

Little happened aside from a few jabs for the first 27 seconds of Round One. Then with 4:33 left—and just as Mir was pointing out that GSP would be better off staying upright and making the match as much about striking as possible—GSP went in for a takedown. It surprised everyone in the building, including Hughes who was on his butt before he knew it. With GSP on top of him and beginning to strike, Hughes jockeyed to find a choke hold position.

Hughes managed to lift both men up onto their feet and began to push GSP backward. Before he hit the fence, GSP was able to slip from Hughes's grip and the two separated. The pair exchanged jabs before GSP threw a huge left roundhouse kick that just barely grazed Hughes's face. A few more blows were thrown by each fighter before Hughes made his own takedown attempt. He pushed GSP up against the fence and was clearly setting up a proper grip to pick him up and throw him down. It took a few tries, but Hughes managed to get GSP airborne and slammed him hard down to the mat in an impressive takedown.

In Hughes's grip, GSP rolled his eyes in obvious frustration. Then he began to twist in an attempt to loosen Hughes's lock. It worked. Although he didn't manage to break Hughes's grip entirely, GSP did actually get back up on his feet. And in a moving clinch, the fighters traded knee shots to the abdomen. As Hughes was attempting another knee, GSP managed to wriggle away and the two were apart again.

GSP then feigned a right punch, which caught Hughes looking, and turned and unloaded a huge spinning kick right onto Hughes's belly. It landed with a very audible thud and sent Hughes stumbling back to the fence. He looked shocked, but recovered quickly and made a takedown attempt that GSP managed to dodge. As he was getting up, GSP threw a massive right cross at him that just missed his face. The pair traded jabs before Hughes's left foot smacked GSP in the chin from below.

The fight ended when, with GSP on his back and Hughes in mount on top, he tried to isolate Hughes's left arm to achieve a kimura. But Hughes spun 180 degrees over GSP and got both of his hands on GSP's right arm. With his right foot under GSP's back and his left leg over his neck, Hughes pulled the arm into a classic arm bar.

It was over. As soon as it was obvious that the arm bar was solid, GSP tapped out. But what he didn't realize was that there was just three-tenths of a second left in the first round.

Hughes stood up, calmly walked over to his corner, high-fived his cornermen, then turned around, leaned down to GSP, spoke to him and gave him a big hug.

As Hughes was being named UFC welterweight champion, GSP hugged him again and then hoisted him onto his shoulders to celebrate.

In the post-fight interview, *E!* reporter Kerri Kasem asked Hughes if he thought he'd get a submission from GSP. "No," he answered. "Georges has got such a good grappling background and he's so strong, I never thought it was a possibility to submit him."

When Kasem asked GSP about the prevailing opinion that he was too young to take on a title fight, he answered: "First of all, I just want to tell you something. Matt Hughes is one of my heroes in mixed martial arts, and fighting him was a big honor for me. I'm not going to lie. I was intimidated. But what you saw tonight was the real Rush, Georges St-Pierre. I was at a hundred percent of my power. I just did a bigger mistake than I usually ever did in training. So what can I say but congratulations Matt."

Nobody booed him then.

*   *   *

The loss to Hughes must have been a huge blow to the super-competitive and previously unbeaten GSP—especially when he realized that if he could have withstood the arm bar for less than a second more, the horn would have ended the round and he would have been able to start again in Round Two. But he didn't take any time off to think about it. Instead, he went right back to work—training. He was spending a lot of time with the Canadian national wrestling team under coaches Rob "The Caveman" Moore and Cleo "Zulu Man" Ncube, honing his skills against Olympians and perhaps thinking about giving the Games a shot himself.

GSP did eventually talk about the bout with Hughes. He had grown up watching Hughes and considered him one of his heroes. Hughes made his professional debut when GSP was just 17, and won his first UFC fight just a year later. The guys GSP had fought before had been young athletes like him, not star fighters he had grown up watching on television. GSP was so intimidated by Hughes, he admitted, that he couldn't even look him directly in the eye.

Despite that remarkable handicap, GSP had actually acquitted himself well. In fact, before the lethal arm bar, the judges looked like they were scoring the round in GSP's favor. Certainly the kick to Hughes's gut that sent his reeling was the obvious highlight of the round before the tap out.

Like a shark, he couldn't stay still and he couldn't go backward. Though no longer the top welterweight contender, he was a respected UFC fighter who had made mixed martial arts fighting his full-time profession. He was well respected. Many observers—both fans and members of the media—had considered GSP the future of the sport and felt that he was too young and inexperienced for a title shot when he fought Hughes. They said that the match proved that theory right. They all knew that GSP would be a champ in the future—and that his diverse skills were the future of UFC fighting.

But—and this is fitting considering his personal philosophy of working hard to win success—he wasn't going to get anything but praise for free. He was going to have to earn another title shot.

His road back to the Promised Land was going to begin in a familiar place—Centre Pierre-Charbonneau—and among familiar faces at *TKO 19: Rage* set for January 29, 2005.

* * *

His opponent would be Dave Strasser. A long-time mixed martial arts veteran with a 21–5–4 record as a professional, the 35-year-old Strasser was considered one of the pioneers of the sport in the United States, but he was almost 34 when he made his UFC debut. For that bout he was matched against Brazilian jiu-jitsu expert Romie Aram. With an impressive physique and a 6–0 professional record, Aram was generating the same kind of buzz as GSP. Because of that, many observers considered the Strasser–Aram fight at *UFC 42: Sudden Impact* to be a warm-up match for Aram on his own way to battle Hughes (or Penn) for the welterweight championship.

But it didn't work out that way. Although Aram did knock Strasser down right away, the veteran managed to turn the fight around. After dominating the young hotshot for three full rounds, leaving him bloody and clearly beaten, Strasser was awarded a unanimous 30–27 decision.

In his prefight interview, Strasser said: "I came all the way from America to Canada to fight Georges St-Pierre." That comment drew the ire of many Canadian fans who pointed out that the two countries share a border, but in Strasser's defense, he lives and trains in Kenosha, Wisconsin, which is nowhere near the Canadian border and is almost 1,000 miles from Montreal. "I don't do much talking," he continued. "I let my fists do the talking."

He looked like a much older man than GSP as he walked down the aisle in a gray hoodie before GSP gamboled out in his blue gi and white headband. It didn't help that his introduction music was Black Sabbath's 1976 hit "Iron Man," which contrasted with GSP's upbeat and very current French-language hip-hop.

There was some booing as Strasser was introduced, but it was drowned out by cheering as soon as the announcer made it clear he was beginning to introduce GSP. Referred to as the Canadian welterweight champion and No. 2-ranked welterweight in the world, GSP bowed to his fans and gave them a double thumbs-up. As he had in the fight against Pete Spratt, GSP wore a GoldenPalace.com henna tattoo. Strasser declined.

Both fighters came out striking. Strasser landed the first blows with his fists and GSP replied with high kicks. It didn't last long. Less than 30 seconds in, Strasser threw a weak left kick. GSP grabbed his leg and forced him onto his back. After just over two minutes of ground-and-pound from side and front mount, GSP found his finisher—GSP wrenched Strasser's arm away from his body. Strasser knew what GSP wanted to do, but could not manage to stop it. Once his arm was bent back to an unbearable angle, he tapped out.

Immediately, GSP did a backflip in celebration. Then he spoke to and hugged Strasser, who was still wincing from the pain of the kimura. GSP then mounted a turnbuckle and held his belt over his head. He followed that up with his traditional break dance routine and posed for some photos. He had rewarded his loyal fans in Montreal, and he had shown he was ready to make another run at the title.

* * *

The era in which GSP was emerging was a watershed time for the UFC. There were still many detractors in the mainstream media. "[It's] violence for the sake of violence," wrote prominent *New York Post* sports columnist Phil Mushnick. "I understand that not everything necessarily has to have a redeeming social value. It can have no value. But this kind of stuff has negative value."

But the public and, perhaps more importantly, people with money and influence were beginning to come around. In June 2004, the UFC signed on as a client with the Creative Artists Agency (CAA), which is generally considered to be the most powerful talent agency in the world, with clients like Steven Spielberg, Brad Pitt, AC/DC and Peyton Manning. Immediately, UFC-themed movie and TV show ideas were circulating around Hollywood.

The result of CAA's efforts was a reality TV show called *The Ultimate Fighter* shown on Spike TV, a basic cable channel owned by Viacom and MTV that is devoted to men's interests and has frequently had its level of maturity questioned in the mainstream media. *The Ultimate Fighter* featured two coaches—in the first season they were Randy Couture and Chuck "The Iceman" Liddell—who presided over four middleweights and four light heavyweights each. The young fighters would face elimination first in athletic challenges and then in the Octagon. The show's narrator was Mike Rowe, the former opera singer and QVC shill who was becoming something of a hot property on basic cable at the time, and it was hosted by Dana White and singer/model Willa Ford.

The winning fighter would be given what the show called a "six-figure contract" to fight in the UFC. But it was more complicated than that. The winner would receive a three-year contract stipulating that he would fight three times a year. In the first year, he would receive $12,000 per fight with a $12,000 bonus for a win. Those figures would escalate to $16,000 in the second year of the contract and $22,000 in the third. With a perfect 9–0 record after three years, the fighter could have made $300,000.

There was no shortage of willing participants. The show premiered on January 17, 2005, and it delivered more action than most reality shows could wish for. There was drunkenness, name-calling, fighting outside the ring, and the odd door bashed in, and one contestant got revenge on another by urinating on his pillow. The combination of controversy and combat clicked with viewers. Despite being on at the same time as USA Network's WWE show, *The Ultimate Fighter* was an immense ratings success. More than 2.6 million viewers saw the final show of the first season—a colossal number for the time.

White claimed it was all part of the master plan. He called it his "Trojan Horse," indicating that it was his way of sneaking his product into mainstream consciousness. It worked. When Spike aired *The Ultimate Fighter I Finale* on April 9, 2005, it drew more viewers than MTV's popular *X Games* or even NFL preseason action on ESPN2, and it did so among the most desirable demographics for advertisers.

Viewers were rewarded by a heck of a show. Many of the old-school fans tuned in to see a headline bout between future UFC hall-of-famer Ken "The World's Most Dangerous Man" Shamrock and up-and-coming Rich "Ace" Franklin rather than the winners of the reality show. Although theirs was a good fight—Franklin was the first opponent ever to knock Shamrock out in his long professional career—it was hardly the best one. That distinction was given to the winners of the light heavyweight competition—Forrest Griffin and Stephan "American Psycho" Bonnar. Their grueling three-round decision was unanimous, but very close. White was so impressed that he offered a UFC contract not just to the winner, Griffin, but to Bonnar as well.

It could not have worked out better for the UFC or come at a better time. Although the fans it already had were very ardent, their number simply wasn't big enough, and it was widely reported that the league was teetering on the brink of bankruptcy. But, as fans of mixed martial arts have always maintained, wider exposure leads to a wider fan base because people who think they won't like mixed martial arts often do once they see it. They appear to have been right. The last UFC event before *The Ultimate Fighter*'s first season aired, *UFC 50: The War of '04*, sold 40,000 pay-per-view subscriptions. The first one after the season finale, *UFC 52: Couture vs. Liddell 2* (which featured the opposing coaches from *The Ultimate Fighter*) sold 280,000—a sevenfold increase in less than five months. Not only was the UFC saved from extinction, it made a profound step toward becoming a mainstream sport.

* * *

It was into this ever more popular UFC that GSP would make his return. The UFC had already announced that GSP was to fight Jason "Mayhem" Miller at *UFC 52: Couture vs. Liddell 2* on

April 16, 2005. But they had also announced that Pete Spratt was going to fight Karo Parisyan at *UFC 46* before he lost to GSP and was replaced by him. Few at the time believed GSP would be on the card at *UFC 52* had he lost to Strasser.

Miller was making his UFC debut, but he had already amassed a significant fan base while earning a 12–3 professional record. While many fighters—like Hughes and GSP himself—attract fans by maintaining modest personalities, Miller used his sense of humor and unpredictability to impress a different type of fan. Playing on his own nickname, he referred to his followers as "Mayhem monkeys." Though more comfortable fighting at 185 pounds, he came down a weight class for the fight because the UFC was actively looking for welterweight challengers, not middleweights.

"My style is a mixture of street fighting, jiu-jitsu, Thai boxing, wrestling," he said with a grin before the fight. "I've got everything you need to be a certified ass-whupper."

In his prefight interview, GSP seemed more confident and less modest than he had in previous fights. As with Miller's, his comments seemed more genuine and less scripted than those he and others typically delivered before UCC/TKO fights. "If I fight to the best of my abilities, if I am 100 percent mentally and physically, I think nobody can handle my rhythm," he said. "Nobody in my weight class—not only Miller—nobody in my weight class." While GSP's English was very good, he still had a strong Québécois accent, and many people—both fans and detractors alike—have used many variations of the phrase "'andle my riddum" to mock or praise GSP over the years.

GSP said he was in the best shape of his life. When asked his prediction, he said, "I will land some big strikes and go for a submission on the ground." When told that Miller accused him of having "no heart" and was predicting a TKO, GSP smiled and said, "I don't think so; we'll see if he is as good a fighter as he is at talking."

Miller made an entrance that would have made Thomas "Wildman" Denny blush. Wearing the same kind of mask that members of Slipknot, the horror metal band that was blaring through the speakers, wear onstage, Miller came out dancing. Then he stopped, removed the mask and started throwing dollar bills into the audience. His wide, goofy grin revealed that his front teeth had been capped not with gold but, perhaps even more gaudily, platinum. He also had a bright red spot dyed into the hair on top of his head.

As is his custom, GSP's walkout music was classic hip-hop, this time DMX's popular "X Gon' Give it to Ya." Dressed in the familiar blue gi and white headband, GSP strode down the aisle as happy-looking as Miller. He threw a few T-shirts with the name Mopai.com (a now-defunct online martial-arts gear supplier) across the front into the crowd before high-fiving his fans. As GSP approached the Octagon, play-by-play announcer Goldberg pointed out that Matt Hughes had just that week told him that GSP was the future of the UFC. He also pointed out that GSP told him that he was not proud of what he had done in the Hughes fight, but that it had forced him to grow up.

The fight began with both fighters moving around the ring with obvious enthusiasm. Miller was hopping around in what he calls his "monkey style," then he started the action with a low, sweeping right leg that failed to connect. The two traded punches to the body with little effect. Miller then went for another right roundhouse, but GSP caught it and sent him tumbling to the canvas.

Miller was on the ground, prepared for a front mount, but instead GSP kicked him in the butt. Then GSP lifted his left leg just over waist height and sent it down on Miller's gut. Many fans at

the time were shocked that GSP was not disqualified for stomp-
ing, but referee John "Big John" McCarthy—a former Los Angeles
police officer who was becoming something of a celebrity in his
own right in mixed martial arts circles—ruled it to be an axe kick
because GSP struck him with the back of his foot, not the bottom.
GSP then went in for a mount, but Miller was too well protected.
They exchanged a few punches, but an obviously frustrated GSP
backed off, allowing Miller to get back on his feet.

Three inches taller than GSP, Miller tried to take advantage of
his superior reach. Miller went on the offensive and managed to
land two hard roundhouses, one from each side. Then they each
landed punches, though GSP's was harder. After a couple more
good shots, GSP made a rare mistake. He threw a spinning back-
hand that Miller easily ducked under. His follow-through allowed
Miller to grab him. Miller was desperate to bring the fight to the
ground, but GSP shook him off again.

Miller then took a kick to the legs before landing a big right
fist on GSP's face. GSP was well bloodied by this point. He landed a monster right before grabbing Miller and forcing him to the
fence. GSP grasped him around the waist and looked like he was
attempting a Matt Hughes–style lift and slam, but succeeded only
in dragging Miller to the canvas.

He started in on the ground-and-pound, but Miller muted the
challenge with his excellent ground game. After much spinning
and twisting, Miller managed to get GSP back up on his feet and
threw him off. GSP eventually went in, hammering Miller with his
fists on his way down. Then GSP took control. He rained dozens
of hard blows on Miller, who was able to do nothing at this point
but try to protect himself. Play-by-play man Goldberg commented
that the amount of blood being spilled may prompt McCarthy to
call the fight.

GSP tried to set up a kimura. The opponents traded blows until GSP took him down with a bull rush. Miller established a rubber guard. GSP nearly established a head-and-arm choke, but Miller—ever resourceful—wriggled out. The reward for his efforts was a series of strikes from GSP's knees, forearms and fists. Time ran out with GSP trying to break Miller's guard.

It was a brutal round that became more one-sided as it went along. Still, Miller got up with a big grin on his face and was still smiling while his cornerman did his best to stop the bleeding from the cut on the bridge of his nose.

In the second round, GSP worked hard to achieve a kimura, but Miller defended himself effectively. As he had before, Miller got on his elbows and knees—a strong defensive posture often called "turtling up" that offers little opportunity for an attacker, but also prevents the defender from doing much of anything else. All GSP could do was knee him in the flank. Miller spun and pulled guard up against the fence. With less than two minutes remaining in the round, GSP was on top of him quickly and slammed him with a big right hand. Miller rolled over again, appearing to turtle up, but he escaped and was up on his feet right away.

Searching for a quick submission before the round ended, GSP began to set up an arm bar. GSP got Miller in a classic arm bar— very similar to how Hughes had beaten GSP earlier—but Miller held out, did not tap, and the horn sounded to end the round.

Miller opened well in Round Three, connecting with a jab to GSP's face. But GSP replied with his own jab that appeared harder and sent Miller back a step. Miller unsuccessfully tried another punch and a kick that began off balance and hit nothing but air. Taking advantage, GSP rushed Miller and took him down quickly.

GSP went into his ground-and-pound routine, landing elbows and fists. But for the first time in the match Miller took the upper hand. He put GSP on his back, went into side mount and landed two quick knees. Calling on his incredible leg strength, GSP managed to turn the tables again, putting Miller on his back. With just a few seconds left, GSP hammered Miller with his fists and knees.

There was no question who had won. Although there was no TKO, it was an absolutely dominating performance by GSP. It confirmed to many that he was ready to rejoin the UFC title hunt. After the fight, GSP seemed confident that he had done well. "It was not the toughest fight of my life," he said. "He's a tough guy and I tried to submit him a couple of times, but he never tapped."

Although he was back in the big time, he wasn't getting the big bucks. While Couture received $150,000 for losing to Liddell (who made $140,000) and Hughes made $110,000 for defending his title against Frank Trigg, GSP pocketed just $18,000 ($9,000 for fighting and another $9,000 for winning).

For GSP, what really counted was that he was back in the big leagues where he belonged. When asked what he wanted next, GSP made it obvious. "For sure, I want to have another shot [at the title]," he said. "I don't know if they're going to give it to me right now—maybe I'm going to have to fight again, maybe a couple of guys—but we'll see what's going to happen. Me, I'm ready for anything."

*   *   *

What came next was not a title shot, but it was still a very good fight with one of the most skilled fighters in the MMA at the time. At *UFC 54: Boiling Point*—held at the MGM Grand Arena in Las Vegas on August 20, 2005—GSP was scheduled to fight Frank "Twinkle Toes" Trigg. Trigg grew up in a not-well-off but loving family in upstate New York. As one of seven brothers, Trigg said he learned how to wrestle out of necessity. He had a talent for it and later excelled at wrestling in both high school and at the University of Oklahoma. After completing his degree in public affairs and administration, he began to study judo under Olympic bronze medalist Patrick Burris. And before long he was fighting professionally for a variety of mixed martial arts organizations.

By the time he was to fight GSP, he had amassed a 12–3 record as a professional. Even more impressive was the fact that two of his three losses had come in close, dramatic fights at the hands of Matt Hughes—one of which Trigg dominated until the end when Hughes slipped into a rear-naked choke and is considered by many the best UFC fight ever—and the other was a come-from-behind victory by Hayato Sakurai in a bout that Trigg had also looked in control of before falling to a series of knees. Despite his nickname, "Twinkle Toes," Trigg clearly had the talent to contend with any welterweight in the world.

Before the fight, Trigg—who is known for trash-talking, often playfully, before fights—played much the same card that Hughes had before he fought GSP. Although he conceded that GSP was a phenomenal fighter and that he was a potential future champion, he also said that he was too young—remember GSP was still just 24 years old—and inexperienced to beat him.

GSP replied to that opinion in a much different way than he had when Hughes espoused it. "For the title, maybe I was not ready mentally to . . . fight for a title," he said. "Now I think I [am] twice as strong as I was before and . . . I think right now it's a good time for me. Mentally . . . I'm a lot stronger than I was; and physically too I've got a lot more tools. And I'm a new fighter right now. [The] loss was the best thing that happened to me. It's made me become a more complete, a stronger fighter physically and mentally."

Trigg started the bout aggressively and kept striking as he led with his right and sent in some jabs with his left. GSP responded with some quick lefts of his own and followed with a right round-house kick. Both fighters continued to trade punches.

GSP began to dominate the ground game as he relentlessly pursued Trigg. Trigg did get on his feet once, but GSP smacked him back down. Back up on his feet, but with his hands on the ground and head down, Trigg was still trying to stand when GSP threw his right leg over him and Trigg collapsed to the mat. With Trigg on his back, GSP managed to get his head and one arm in a triangle choke. While he was still struggling, Trigg's face was turning visibly purple. But before GSP could fully lock in the triangle choke, he lost it. Trigg started to breathe deeply again, but GSP landed a few big hits to his face. Trigg struggled underneath, trying to find a way out. There were more than two minutes left in Round One, and GSP's strikes—particularly his left elbow—were doing more and more damage. Trigg made another unsuccessful escape attempt. Then he got back up on his hands and feet with GSP still on top. As GSP kept hammering, Trigg fell to his elbows and was using his head to keep himself up. His legs started to shake under the weight. They gave out and he went back to his knees.

Trigg looked beaten as the clock showed a minute left. He was on his elbows and knees, his hands behind his neck. But as GSP started to throw a huge punch, Trigg showed he had some fight left in him. He got up on his knees and—in a flash—fell over onto GSP. But GSP rolled them over, and this time GSP had his arms around Trigg's throat. After a few seconds of rear-naked choke, Trigg tapped out. The second the ref called it, GSP went into a running backflip.

The fight was an instant wake-up call to the mixed martial arts community—fans and fighters alike. The stats could hardly have been more one-sided. Thirty-seven of 44 strike attempts (25 of 32 significant strikes), succeeded in his only takedown attempt, recorded 10 passes and won by submission with 51 seconds remaining in the first round. Trigg landed just one of three strikes and failed in his only takedown attempt.

After the fight, GSP said that his strategy in the fight was to go for the takedown right away—even though conventional wisdom before the fight was that GSP would be better off standing—because he thought Trigg was "not as effective on his back as he is on top." He also revealed that he thought he was worthy of another shot at the title, and he wanted to fight Hughes in particular.

His pay packet was getting heavier. He earned $28,000 that night ($13,000 to fight and $15,000 for the win). But it paled in comparison to Randy Couture's, even though his light heavyweight bout was not for a belt and his opponent was 40-year-old Mike van Arsdale, who was never considered a true contender. Couture's popularity and the publicity generated by *The Ultimate Fighter* paid off. He took home $225,000 that night ($150,000 to fight and $75,000 for the win).

*   *   *

No matter how convincing GSP was against Trigg, the UFC did not think he was ready for another shot at the title just yet. Instead, he was matched up against respected veteran Sean "The Muscle Shark" Sherk at *UFC 56: Full Force* on November 19, 2005.

A natural-born wrestler from small-town Minnesota, Sherk discovered martial arts in his late teens and studied boxing, shoot wrestling and muay Thai before competing in his first mixed martial arts fight. He compiled an incredible 17–0–1 record in a variety of organizations (including the UFC and UCC and, notably, notched two of his wins against Parisyan) before facing Hughes for the UFC welterweight title at *UFC 42: Sudden Impact* in Miami on April 25, 2003.

He put up a great fight, going the distance in the bout, but the judges favored Hughes. It was Sherk's first professional loss. He then left the UFC, recording 12 straight wins in a number of other organizations and building a huge fan base in Japan, before returning to take on GSP at *UFC 56*.

Hughes was then scheduled to fight Parisyan to defend his title, but a torn hamstring sidelined Parisyan. Later, he would become addicted to the prescription painkillers he was given after the injury and, in 2009, be suspended from professional fighting for nine months.

The UFC quickly found a replacement. Joe "Diesel" Riggs started boxing as a child and was a star wrestler at the same Glendale, Arizona, high school Couture wrestled for before discovering Brazilian jiu-jitsu. He started fighting professionally in the autumn of 2001, and compiled an impressive 23–6–0 record with one no contest before *UFC 56*. He began his career as a light heavyweight, slimmed down to a middleweight in the spring of 2004 and made his debut in the UFC at *UFC 55: Fury* as a welterweight, beating Chris "Lights Out" Lytle with a TKO brought on by cuts two minutes into the second round.

But, as luck would have it, Riggs failed to make weight for *UFC 56*. He was less than a pound over, but it still meant that his fight against Hughes would not be a title bout.

Even more controversial than the events surrounding the Hughes fight was the bombshell UFC president Dana White dropped before anybody took the ring. He announced that the UFC and BJ Penn had reached a settlement and that the former champion would be returning to contend for the welterweight title. That was especially big news for GSP. Earlier in the day he could have considered himself the rightful No. 2 welterweight in the world, but with Penn back in the running, he was rather obviously pushed back to No. 3.

In the prefight interviews, neither Sherk nor GSP said much that wasn't predictable. But David Loiseau, a fellow fighter from Montreal who was also GSP's long-time training partner and cornerman, said: "We're going to impose Georges's rhythm right off the bat and . . . see if he can follow it. Georges is going to keep his hands up, his chin down and isn't going to walk into anything, but impose his style right off the bat." While he was talking, he was rubbing GSP's ears and face.

Instead of the inspirational American hip-hop he had previously used as entrance music, GSP entered to a different type of tune. Neg' Marrons is a dancehall ragga band from France made up of members from former French colonies in Africa (Congo and Cape Verde) and the Caribbean (Martinique). GSP had long been a fan and picked their song "Tout Le Monde Debout" (Everybody Stand Up) as his entrance music. His boxer-style shorts had his nickname "Rush" and two versions of Spike TV's logo on them.

Sherk, about eight years older, chose "Wait," a somber song from alternative metal band Earshot. His baseball cap and hoodie also contrasted sharply with GSP's bright-red, sponsor-laden gi and white headband.

GSP looked positively huge compared to the 5-foot-6 Sherk. But Sherk looked thicker, more chiseled and, once the fight began, quicker and more aggressive. Rogan, the color commentator, assessed the situation, saying: "This easily could be a title fight." No more than a second into the match, Sherk came charging in with a low, sweeping right kick that failed to connect. GSP threw a big left kick that just missed, but he managed a right punch on the follow-through.

GSP made a takedown, but Sherk reacted quickly, setting up a butterfly guard. Before Sherk could attempt a sweep, GSP pulled away and Sherk stumbled backward, eventually finding his feet.

After the two exchanged punches, Sherk dove under GSP's fists and grabbed his legs in a takedown attempt. GSP managed to maintain his footing by sprawling wide with his legs and Sherk slid off him.

Then they were boxing again, with Sherk kicking low and GSP kicking high. One high kick connected, thrilling the fans. Referee Herb Dean stopped the action to see if Sherk was okay after the kick and after Sherk grinned and stuck both his thumbs up, Dean restarted the action.

Both fighters started striking with fists and kicks. Again, Sherk's kicks were low and GSP's were high. Sherk landed one very powerful left hook, but GSP was getting the better of the exchange. While Sherk was sending his fist at GSP's head, the taller man dove under for a spectacular takedown, slamming Sherk into the fence, then down to the canvas.

On the ground, Sherk was struggling while GSP was landing his right fist repeatedly. After a few moments, Sherk unleashed his own set of punches. GSP stopped them by getting in close, but that allowed Sherk to lock his hands around the back of GSP's chest.

On his feet for more leverage, GSP pushed Sherk back down. Pounding his face relentlessly, first with his fists and then later—and more powerfully—with his forearms and elbows, GSP seemed in complete control. The horn sounded just as GSP landed a big right to Sherk's face. GSP sprung to his feet, backed away from Sherk and went to his corner.

The second round started much like the first, with Sherk aggressively attacking with low kicks and long punches. They kept boxing and kicking for a while, with GSP landing one particularly strong kick to Sherk's midsection and another spinning back kick that sent Sherk back a few feet. But it was a punch—a big left hook—that sent Sherk stumbling, nearly to the ground. He recovered quickly, but GSP delivered a high kick that he had to duck almost as soon as he was up. As Sherk was getting ready to box, GSP lunged under his fists and pushed him back. Sherk was hopping on one leg until his back was slammed into the fence.

Once on the ground, it was back to the now-familiar ground-and-pound. GSP was hammering Sherk with both elbows and fists and started him bleeding. Play-by-play man Mike Goldberg noted that Sherk had "a look of extreme pain on his face" and opined that he thought his nose might be broken. Herb Dean came in for a closer look. Once satisfied Sherk should not continue, he stopped the fight.

GSP had completed his victory backflip before Sherk had even gotten off the canvas.

After the fight, Sherk talked about how he tried to stay upright because nobody expected it of him and he had been training for it. He complimented GSP on his ability to resist takedowns with his sprawl and said, "He was very, very slippery . . . must've had some oil on or something . . . I couldn't grab him for nothing." That was a serious accusation. Cornermen keep Vaseline on hand to treat cuts and abrasions fighters suffer in the ring, and that is perfectly legal under UFC rules. But Vaseline or any other lubricant can give a fighter an immense advantage if it is applied in any amount on the body. Because grappling and takedowns require traction, a greased fighter would be almost immune to them. But Sherk stepped back a little, and didn't want to say GSP cheated to win. "All excuses aside," he said, wiping blood from his now puffed-up nose, "the guy has great sprawl, hits hard, moves well . . . so it was a great fight but I really wanted to win, so, if my hand isn't raised, I'm not happy about the outcome."

GSP was all smiles. "At the end of the fight when he was down and I was hitting him, I heard 'ahh!' so I know he was hurt, so

I kept going, I finished him," he said. While he was being interviewed, GSP saw on a TV that Hughes was being interviewed in the ring. Hughes had just finished off Riggs with a first-round kimura. GSP brought the reporters over to the TV. "Maybe he will say something about me," he said, grinning broadly. "I would like to fight this guy—I really like him as a person, as a fighter, he's one of my idols. And I would like to have a rematch with this guy. It's very important for me to have a rematch. This is a very phenomenal guy; according to me, he is the biggest champion in the UFC. If I could beat this guy, it would be a huge achievement for me."

It was a big win by any standard. Sherk was a very, very formidable opponent, and GSP took it to him, winning by TKO by cumulative strikes at 2:53 of the second round. The stats look like the one-sided boxing match that it was. GSP landed 78 of 132 strikes (58 of 111 significant ones) as compared to Sherk's 32 of 67 (20 of 55). GSP was successful on three of four takedown attempts, while Sherk failed on all three of his.

The fight solidified GSP's legitimacy as a contender for the welterweight crown. And it paid a little better, too. GSP received $16,000 for fighting and an additional $19,000 for winning, for a total of $35,000. For the main event, Hughes received $110,000 ($55,000 each for fighting and winning).

Clearly, it paid to be welterweight champ, and GSP wanted it more than anything else in the world. He wanted to fight Hughes, not just so he could be world champion, but also to avenge the only loss of his professional career.

* * *

But the UFC did not pay attention to GSP's wishes. It wouldn't have made sense. With BJ Penn back in the organization, it would be more exciting and far more lucrative to pit GSP and Penn against each other to determine which fighter would challenge Hughes.

Penn would be an even more strenuous test than Trigg or even Sherk. Born and raised in Hawaii, Jay Dee Penn was the youngest of four brothers. Three of the four were named Jay Dee Penn, after their father—the other was named Reagan—so they were given nicknames to differentiate them. Since he was the youngest, he earned the nickname "Baby Jay," which was later shortened to BJ.

Penn began studying Brazilian jiu-jitsu at the suggestion of a neighbor when he was 17, and he enjoyed it so much that he moved to California two years later to study under Ralph Gracie.

He was lured to the UFC in 2001 and recorded a 7–1–1 record as a professional, including the win over Hughes and one fight with Hawaii's *Rumble on the Rock* promotion, before the disagreement with White sent him out of the organization. During the two-year hiatus from the UFC, Penn fought for K-1 in Japan and Hawaii, winning three bouts, including a three-round decision against middleweight Rodrigo Gracie, Ralph's nephew.

Back in the UFC, he was as eager to win back the welterweight title as GSP was to snatch it from Hughes. Their fight would be a matchup fans were dying to see—though oddly not the main event—of *UFC 58: USA vs. Canada*. Held at the Mandalay Bay venue in Las Vegas on March 4, 2006, the gimmick behind *UFC 58* was that all eight fights pitted an American against a Canadian. The main event featured GSP's friend and training partner David Loiseau, who would face Cincinnati's Rich Franklin, a scholar who earned a master's degree in mathematics and was a teacher before becoming an MMA professional.

Before the fight, GSP did his best to convince reporters that he wouldn't be starstruck by Penn. "If I wasn't fighting him, he would probably be one of my favorite fighters," he said. "But this time, I won't make the same mistake I made with Hughes, I will fight him like I fight everyone else." To be prepared for Penn's technically proficient ground game, GSP wisely decided to train at Renzo Gracie's academy in New York City.

It was clear that GSP was a different person than the excitable, gum-chewing boy he had been in 2003. Now just shy of 25, GSP was calm and confident in front of cameras, answering in near-perfect English—his accent now more charming than obscurant—and with measured, well-formulated sentences.

Despite GSP's protests that he was not to be overwhelmed by Penn's celebrity, Penn cunningly played a psychological card. Walking out to his favorite Hawaiian hip-hop band, Sudden Rush, Penn wore his UFC title belt—he had refused to give it up when White stripped him of the title—and a T-shirt emblazoned with two words: World Champ. Before the fight, he made his opinion about his status very clear, saying: "I know I'm the welterweight champ, Matt Hughes knows it, and Dana knows it." He looked pudgy compared to chiseled fighters like GSP and Hughes, but as a natural 155-pounder fighting in the 170-pound class, he had to cut less weight than most welterweights.

Unlike many of GSP's fights, there was no taking time to size the other guy up. Penn started punching within the first second of action, and GSP followed suit and added a high kick that missed Penn's face. GSP then connected with a low kick, but it left him open to two nasty punches to the head. After about 15 seconds of spirited boxing from both fighters, GSP sent in another low kick.

Although GSP had his fans there, the bulk of the crowd was vocally behind Penn. After taking a few more punches to the head, GSP began to close his right eye and it quickly became evident he was bleeding. Penn went in for a huge punch, GSP answered with a quick left that sent him reeling, but Penn quickly recovered.

GSP was now also bleeding from the nose. That's not good for a fighter. If he can't breathe through his nose, a fighter has to keep his mouth open, which is a major disadvantage when receiving strikes to the head and could lead to a knockout that wouldn't have happened if his mouth was closed because the jaw is less protected. He landed a few jabs and a nice inside kick that almost took Penn's leg out from under him. After a few similar exchanges, GSP slammed Penn with a spinning leg kick and followed it with a glancing high kick.

GSP then threw a hard right cross that Penn ducked and used to grab GSP around the chest. The men both exchanged a series of knees as GSP walked a willing Penn to the fence. With a big part of the crowd chanting "BJ! BJ!" GSP tried various holds and lock set-ups on Penn, but couldn't get anything to stick. Finally, he bent at the waist, grabbed Penn's left leg with both arms and started lifting. Penn hopped on his right foot back over to the fence for balance and broke GSP's hold.

After a couple of punches and knees from both men, Penn broke the clinch and hit GSP squarely in the face with a hard jab. GSP came out kicking, but just barely connected. The round ended with the pair in a clinch.

Aside from his regrettable submission to Hughes, it was the worst round GSP had yet recorded as a professional. Although he landed a few blows, he came out of the round bloody and looking both tired and overmatched.

When the second round began, GSP's nose had not stopped bleeding, despite the efforts of his cornermen. This time, though, it was GSP who came out quickly and aggressively, throwing a number of punches right away and a nice left high kick that Penn barely blocked. He had been hammering away at Penn's left calf throughout the first round and continued with this strategy, which is painful and potentially immobilizing. He landed his first punch, but Penn hopped over the second. Back in a clinch, GSP walked Penn back to the fence while exchanging knees again. And, just as in Round One, GSP grabbed Penn's left thigh in a takedown attempt.

It was long and tortuous, with a lot of one-legged hopping by Penn, but GSP finally took him down. Penn set up an excellent guard quickly and the two were soon trading small punches. Penn took his feet from GSP's hips and used a closed guard. Unable to break his guard or switch to a side mount, GSP let go and stood up.

They were back in a clinch when GSP grabbed Penn around the backs of the thighs, lifted him off the ground and slammed him to the mat. But with just 14 seconds left in the round, there was little he could get accomplished. The horn sounded and GSP got off Penn. His face was now covered in blood. He later told a reporter that his vision was so bad, it looked to him as if he were fighting three Penns. But that, he said, only made him more aggressive.

With the score essentially even at one round apiece, Round Three began with GSP coming out aggressively. For the third time, GSP clinched up and marched Penn backward to the fence. GSP grabbed Penn's right thigh again, but with Penn leaned against the fence, slipped and fell to his knees on the takedown attempt. But he regained his footing, put both arms under Penn's thighs and—much to the crowd's astonishment—lifted him up, carried him a few steps and slammed him to the canvas.

With the action so close that the blood from GSP's face was smeared all over Penn's chest, the two grappled with little conclusiveness. Eventually, Penn managed to spin and get to his feet. Both men looked tired as they clinched once again on the fence.

Back in the center of the Octagon, Penn rushed GSP and got his arms behind his thighs. He managed to get his feet off the ground as he drove him back toward the fence, but not down. Up against the fence, Penn slipped his leg behind GSP's and hooked it off the ground. Both men went down, but not all the way. Using the fence for support, GSP landed on his knees. Penn concentrated all his efforts on GSP's right leg, so GSP used his hands and left leg to get back up to standing.

Back in the clinch, GSP spun them around so that Penn's back was against the fence again. Penn slid his knee up far enough to use it to push GSP off him for a brief boxing match, but GSP dove back in almost immediately.

With about a minute left, Penn pushed him off again. As he approached GSP to throw a punch, Penn found that GSP had grabbed his right thigh. In an instant he was on his back with GSP back on top of him. Penn then—without the use of his hands—looped his left leg around GSP's right arm. Then he grabbed it to tighten the hold. He then started hitting GSP until GSP returned with a huge left. With just a few seconds left, he tried to accomplish the same feat with his right leg, but GSP blocked it and, after a few seconds, squirmed out of his other leg hold.

The horn sounded with GSP on top. Hughes and White stood up to applaud, and the audience followed suit, giving the fighters a long and rare standing ovation. Although Goldberg said he'd "hate to have to judge this fight" and Rogan added that GSP "just may have pulled it out," the fighters looked like they thought they knew who'd won. GSP was jubilant, hugging his cornermen (though in no shape for a backflip), while Penn looked worried and somber.

Nelson Hamilton scored it 29–28 GSP. Cecil Peoples scored it 29–28 Penn. And Marco Rosales scored it 29–28 GSP. He had won by a split decision. Hughes nodded in agreement. GSP immediately jumped into the air, then walked over to Penn. He lifted Penn's arm up into the air, then hugged him.

After the fight, Penn was disappointed, but conciliatory. "He fought good, he kept pushing," he said. "I should have been going for more takedowns, probably. I thought I did more damage, but he stayed more busy."

"I got cut in the first round," GSP said. "I was more worried about the shoot [takedown attempt], and did not worry about his boxing." He continued, "I made a mistake, but I'm going to learn from it. I knew I was stronger than him, so I tried to make this fight more physical." Laying on the floor with an absorbent cotton ball in each nostril and an ice pack on his head, GSP joked: "I hope not all my fights are like that . . . or I'll have a short career."

Later that night, GSP went to a nearby hospital. "Just as a precaution," he said.

While it was a good night for GSP, it didn't go nearly so well for Loiseau. He was easily handled by Franklin for the first of what would be three straight losses. He continues to fight, even sometimes in the UFC, but hasn't come within sniffing distance of a title shot to this day. Overall, the Americans beat the Canadians 5–3.

It was a lucrative event for GSP. For the first time in his UFC career, he was the top moneymaker at the event, with $48,000 in his pocket. Even so, that was small change compared to the $250,000 Chuck Liddell made at *UFC 57: Liddell vs. Couture 3*. But Liddell was a TV star, and a champ. The kind of guy whose name was put on the event to draw fans. GSP wasn't any of those things yet, but he was doing his best to earn a chance to be all of them.

It wouldn't be easy.

CHAPTER 7

It should have been an opportunity to bask in the limelight, but it wasn't. The euphoria of beating BJ Penn to earn a title fight quickly faded due to two factors. Although there were posters and TV commercials promoting a Matt Hughes-GSP title fight at *UFC 63,* a severe groin injury GSP suffered during training on August 2, 2006, forced him to withdraw from the fight. GSP went to some very highly regarded specialists, but couldn't heal in time for the fight.

Not surprisingly, Penn was asked to take his place, and the event—to be held at the Arrowhead Pond in Anaheim, California, on September 23—was renamed *UFC 63: Hughes vs. Penn.* Many UFC fans were confused because TV commercials featuring a Hughes–GSP match continued to air up until very close to the date of the fight itself.

The other problem GSP had at the time was that Hughes—one of his fighting heroes—was saying things that some, GSP included, took as disrespectful. After finding out that GSP was sidelined, Hughes said he was delighted to be taking on Penn again. "Now

I've got something to really look forward to. I've already beat Georges and here I get to fight BJ Penn, a guy who's beaten me," he said. "I'm a month out and I can really concentrate on BJ Penn now, and I'm looking forward to it."

It's reasonable that Hughes would want revenge on the man who had beaten him rather than face someone he'd already beaten, but Hughes was also said to have commented about how he thought French people were cowards and Canadians were natural pacifists, so it would be a shame to lose to a fighter who was both. That put GSP's nose seriously out of joint. Asked by a French-Canadian reporter if he had any respect for Hughes, GSP replied harshly:

> I used to, but in the last year he said things that were personal and for that he lost all of my respect and that's where Matt Hughes made his mistake and will lose the fight [against me]. He insulted me because I am French, that French people are yellow, French people did not go to war and we were cowards, mentioned that Americans hate and cannot lose to a Canadian . . . All that put together . . . well, he is just another piece of meat where I will do my job this time and not see the guy I used to look up to.

It appeared as though Hughes was in danger of carelessly letting his psychological advantage over the young upstart from Saint Isidore fall away.

* * *

By the time *UFC 63* arrived, Hughes had further enhanced his reputation by beating the legendary Royce Gracie. At *UFC 60: Hughes vs. Gracie*—the most widely watched UFC event to that date with

14,765 people in the seats of the Staples Center in Los Angeles and 620,000 pay-per-view subscriptions—Hughes scored a TKO at the end of Round One after nearly breaking Gracie's arm with a kimura earlier in the round. Of course, Gracie was a few months shy of his 40th birthday and hadn't fought in the UFC in more than 11 years, but he still had star power and added a huge amount of cachet to Hughes's already impressive reputation. Hughes was paid $55,000 for the match, while Gracie—because of his legendary status since *UFC 1*—took home $400,000, or nearly $100,000 for every minute of getting beaten up.

Both Hughes and Penn played their respective roles before their *UFC 63* match. Hughes portrayed himself as chastised by his earlier loss to Penn and ready to take the younger fighter—whom he described as immature and overconfident—to school. For his part, Penn characterized his opponent as an aging one-trick pony who could never keep up with his youth and arsenal of varied moves.

The fight was worth the hype. An accidental poke to the eye forced doctors to check Hughes in the middle of the first round, but he acquitted himself quite well, appearing to win the round by sheer determination. But Penn clearly took the second round—which was mainly on the ground—despite failing to succeed on a rear-naked choke, a triangle choke and an arm bar in rapid succession. But Hughes came out for the third round with renewed aggression. After landing some tough shots, he took Penn to the mat and delivered a flurry of unanswered blows to Penn's face. Referee "Big John" McCarthy had seen enough and stopped the fight. The fight was scored TKO from punches for Hughes at 3:53 of the third round.

Hughes had successfully defended his title once again. And Penn had solidified his post as no better than No. 3 on the list of welterweights. After the fight, all eyes were on No. 2, the only man in the world with a legitimate hope of dethroning Hughes—GSP.

GSP, of course, was there. Unbidden, he stood up and approached the Octagon. Wearing street clothes—including a long-sleeved T-shirt from Tristar, his home gym in Montreal—he came into the Octagon and hugged Hughes, patting him on the back. The crowd cheered his presence loudly.

He gestured to Joe Rogan, who was about to interview Hughes, to let him have the microphone. Up until this point, GSP had never said anything that was at all ungentlemanly or disparaging to other fighters in public. He had developed a strong fan base by being exactly the opposite of the braggarts and loudmouths that had turned so many people off—and even the most anti-GSP UFC fans had to admit that he appeared to be a model citizen. Everything he had said and done had been perfectly admirable, even charming—until he took the microphone from Rogan after *UFC 63*. With Hughes looking at him, GSP smiled at the man he at least said he considered to be a friend and said, "I'm very glad you won that fight, Matt, but I'm not impressed by your performance and I look forward to fight[ing] you in the near future." Then he shook hands with a visibly befuddled and insulted Hughes.

If the crowd was loud in its positive greeting for GSP when he walked in, it was absolutely deafening with its negativity after he spoke. Rogan handed the microphone back to Hughes and asked him what he thought. "That's his opinion," he said. "It might stink, but it's his opinion."

It's not clear whether GSP immediately regretted his actions or not—he was still smiling even after the boos stopped—but he certainly did later. And later that night, he went to see Hughes in the fighters' dressing room.

He grabbed Hughes and told him he had something important to say. Hughes agreed to listen. With his hand on Hughes's shoulder, GSP said: "Look, I apologize. I misunderstood. I thought you were talking shit about me because everybody [he made a beckoning gesture] told me 'come, come, come.' So I thought you were talking shit about me. It's not right what I did and I apologize like a man. But I still want your belt."

By the last sentence the two were shaking hands and grinning. Everyone in the room laughed. GSP did not wait for Hughes to reply. One of Hughes's people yelled, "Get in line, Georges!"

For his part, Hughes seemed assuaged by GSP's sincerity. He told a reporter: "After I won the fight and I was in the locker room, he came in there and wanted to apologize because he thought that I was talking about him out there . . . He was just misunderstood. I mean, I like Georges, he's a great guy. He is . . . He would be a great champion. If I would happen to lose to somebody, I would much rather it be Georges than BJ."

Apology or not, the phrase "not impressed" would find its way into the popular media.

In 2008, a mixed martial arts fan and part-time musician named Derek Greser released a song called "Not Impressed" that features GSP quotes like "I'm not impressed by your performance" and "my ape technique puts people down" set to a simple techno beat. Although it makes fun of GSP's accent and signature giggle, it also points out, quite respectfully, that he is a great fighter. The video has had almost a half-million views on YouTube and has even been heard in a few gyms and dance clubs. Many fighters use it as their workout music, and GSP himself is said to enjoy it.

And in 2010, Asylum.com—an online men's magazine—hired GSP to make a comedic promotional video in which he wanders around their office telling employees that he's "not impressed" by their performances. At the time of writing, it has been seen nearly 200,000 times on YouTube.

Although he has referred to it as his biggest professional re-gret—even including submitting to Hughes when there was less than a second left in the first round—his offhanded and later retracted statement about not being impressed with Hughes's per-formance against Penn did become perhaps GSP's most widely known catchphrase.

*   *   *

Even though he was welterweight champ again, the myth of Hughes was beginning to unravel—at least the concept that he was a simple, likeable and innocent country boy. He was chosen to be a coach (pitted against Rich Franklin) for *The Ultimate Fighter 2*. While his team was much better than Franklin's, this was the first time the mainstream media showed Hughes at any length in an unscripted format, and he came off as self-centered, immature and even a little bit abusive. It was a cold shock to many of his fans.

And when it was obvious that he would fight Hughes for the title, GSP was asked to participate in *The Ultimate Fighter 4*. Still held in a large Las Vegas mansion, the format was changed from two coaches facing off to two teams with a number of trainers whose authority was more limited. This allowed more UFC fighters to get air time. There were also other changes. Instead of a three-year, nonguaranteed contract, the winners were given a shot at the title with a $100,000 purse and a $100,000 sponsorship deal with Xyience, a company that makes UFC-licensed energy drinks and muscle-building supplements. This time the contestants were not unknowns from regional organizations like TKO; they had fought in the UFC at least once and were looking to return. One of the welterweights was Pete Spratt.

The fighters formed two teams—Team No Love and Team Mojo. GSP worked with both, but seemed to favor Team Mojo, which featured his close friend and training partner, Rimouski, Quebec–native Patrick "The Predator" Côté. Côté had started his mixed martial arts career after a stint in the Canadian military, and had amassed an 8–3 record as a professional. But the middleweight was 0–3 in the UFC, losing to Tito Ortiz, Canadian Joe Doerkson and Chris "The Crippler" Leben.

Right from the start, Team Mojo showed more cohesion and a better attitude. Welterweight Matt "The Terror" Serra quickly emerged as a leader and spokesman for them and won over many fans when he served as a cornerman for his teammate Shonie Carter, despite the fact that the two men had a bitter rivalry since Carter had knocked Serra out cold in his UFC debut at *UFC 31: Locked & Loaded* back in 2001. Many fans found Serra's frank attitude, obvious leadership skills and accent entertaining.

GSP made his presence known early, accusing Team No Love of being lazy when they took a day off while he put Team Mojo through very rigorous workouts. Things got really interesting when the fighters gathered to watch the Hughes–Royce Gracie fight, and GSP joined them. A few boos were heard in the room when Hughes was introduced, and when he totally dominated Gracie there were more than a few shocked faces, including GSP's and Serra's; the who had studied under the Gracies for years. Serra vowed to "take [Hughes] out" (perhaps not realizing he was assuming Hughes would beat GSP when they met), and left the room.

Later, GSP would take the members of Team Mojo to a local YMCA to break the routine. But it was too much of a break for one of the fighters. Middleweight Jeremy "Scorpion" Jackson— who had already admitted that his financial troubles had led to his sleeping in his car before he was chosen for the show—met a woman and was kicked off the show for sneaking out later that night to meet up with her. Surveillance video caught him hopping the compound's fence. (His career would later be put in serious jeopardy when he faced a set of charges alleging forcible rape, aggravated assault with a weapon and kidnapping in relation to a 2009 incident. Jackson pleaded guilty to one count of forcible rape and is sentenced on February 14, 2011.)

For much of the competition, GSP looked great. He was polite, supportive, knowledgeable and spoke like an expert. He was a little biased toward Côté, but that surprised no one because they were old friends and training partners.

Things changed about halfway through the competition. The door to the training facility opened and the man behind it was none other than Matt Hughes. He had arrived as an unannounced trainer. The fighters were delighted to see him, but the shock was evident on GSP's face. Hughes shook his hand and said, "What's up, Georgie?" Then, while Hughes was glad-handing the rest of the cast, GSP looked on from a distance with what may well have been a forced smile.

Later, GSP made a big deal about introducing Hughes. Hughes made fun of his hat. Côté pointed out that GSP felt strange with Hughes in the room and when GSP begged out of a training session, Côté asked him if it was because of Hughes. GSP denied it. But he told the cameras: "I'm the No. 1 contender for the welterweight title, so I don't want to be in the same room as Matt Hughes. I don't want to be friends with him, I don't want to share any techniques with him, so I leave the training center."

When he left, Hughes told him he'd "take care of your job for you" and told the fighters they didn't need GSP. In the few moments they were on screen together, Hughes looked calm, and GSP looked awkward. And every time Hughes arrived unannounced, GSP quietly and quickly made an exit.

The simmering tension came to a head after the semifinals, when Hughes decided to treat the fighters and trainers to dinner at Hamada of Japan, a nice restaurant not far from the compound. GSP, who had been laughing and joking with the other guys, immediately turned dour when he saw Hughes enter. Hughes walked over and took a seat across the room from GSP.

He held a schedule up over his head, and spoke loudly to GSP. "Since you're avoiding me, do you want the blue team or the gray team today? And I'll take the opposite tomorrow," he said. "Do you want me to show up or stay away . . ."

GSP's face dropped, but he quickly recovered his grin. "Show up if you want," he replied. "We can roll a little bit."

"Teach me something," Hughes challenged.

"On one condition," GSP joked. "If you teach me one, too."

"The defense of the arm bar?" Hughes said, his words dripping with sarcasm.

The two then laughed it off, but the frustration was clear in GSP's face. The man sitting across from GSP—welterweight Din "The Dinyero" Thomas, who had gained the respect of fans and fighters alike for his outspoken, but astute, observations—said directly to him what many others were thinking: "Kick his ass."

"I seen you, Din!" shouted Hughes.

"I didn't say nothing!" shouted Thomas, laughing.

"It's not like you have little tiny lips," Hughes shouted back, smiling, but not seeming jocular at all. While much of what Hughes said was tasteless, his half-joke about African-American Thomas's lips bordered on offensive. "I can see those lips moving around."

In his 2008 autobiography, Hughes recalled the incident:

Whenever I walked into the room at the training center, Georges walked right out of it. Finally I cornered him at the sushi restaurant. "Georges, what practice do you want to come to and I'll go to the other one?" I couldn't stop thinking about that old joke about Canadian army rifles on sale: Never fired, dropped once. I thought, "I would not want this guy by my side in combat, or outnumbered by thugs. It's one thing to be tough in a cage with a ref, but another thing when you're in a street fight in an alley."

Back in the van on the way home, Serra voiced his opinion, one that the other fighters were quick to agree with. "What a dick," he said. "When he said that, the first thing that popped into my mind was 'what a penis.' Hey, I've got an idea: why don't you go fuck yourself? It's just my idea, whatever. So when you get the belt, do you have a licence to be a penis? Go do your bench presses, ya jerkoff. Fuck you, farmboy." Delivered with impeccable comic timing and an endearing bridge-and-tunnel accent, Serra's little soliloquy was a highlight of the season. The others, particularly Côté, laughed heartily.

Later on, Serra was asked about the incident again. As before, he did not mince words. "At the sushi place, he was trying to dig at Georges a little bit," he said. "And Georges is just, like, a nice guy. I don't know if he's trying to get into his head, but I think he just comes across as a dick."

Whatever Hughes was planning, it backfired. If he was trying to win over people to his side, it had the opposite effect. Serra was not alone in his criticism of Hughes, just the most vociferous. The fighters—and presumably many of the fans—were so disgusted by Hughes and his school yard bully antics that they planted themselves firmly in GSP's camp. If he was trying to gain a psychological edge over GSP for their upcoming fight, he could not have done anything worse. He failed to grasp the basic—and perhaps only—reason he had beaten GSP before. Back then, GSP was in awe of Hughes, thought the world of him, even carried him on his shoulders after he beat him. But now it was clear that GSP had no respect for Hughes, no fear of looking him in the eye and certainly would not hold anything back in their next fight. Any mental edge Hughes had before had been effectively squandered.

The show went along with other minor controversies, including Hughes trying hard to instigate a fight between Serra and coach Marc Laimon over Laimon's criticisms of Royce Gracie. But GSP kept looking admirable. In the middleweight finale, his friend Côté submitted to early favorite Travis "The Serial Killer" Lutter. And, of course, things were more interesting in the welterweight class. Although Hughes predicted he wouldn't get past Carter in the semifinal, Serra won the right to face highly favored Chris "Lights Out" Lytle, then beat him in a controversial split decision. That not only won him the contest and lots of money, but also a shot at the welterweight title at *UFC 69*. He would face Hughes, whom he clearly thought was a dick, or GSP, who he admired a great deal.

* * *

It was a very different UFC and a very different GSP after *The Ultimate Fighter 4*. The success of the TV show—and the data recorded from the long-established TV research methods—gave the UFC a much better idea of what people wanted. And one of the things they learned was that people really wanted to see GSP fight Matt Hughes.

Because of that fact, the main event at *UFC 65: Bad Intentions* was the welterweight championship fight even though there was a heavyweight championship bout between bankable stars Tim Sylvia and Jeff "The Snowman" Monson at the same fight. The date was set for November 18, 2006, and the venue was the massive

ARCO Arena in Sacramento, California, home of the NBA's Kings.

Significantly, the announcement of the fight was made in Toronto. Ontario was by then a lucrative market, but mixed martial arts fights were still illegal. And since the rest of Canada had—on a per-capita basis—been even more receptive to the UFC than the United States, Brazil, Japan or any other country, it made sense for White to stir up fans there in order to pressure the provincial government to change its mind—which eventually happened thanks to effective lobbying.

Before the fight, the UFC spliced two admittedly adversarial interviews to demonstrate the war of words between Hughes and GSP.

Hughes: After I saw BJ and Georges, I said I wasn't impressed by either one of them. Then he jumps in the Octagon and says the same thing about me.

GSP: What I said to Matt Hughes was true; I was not impressed by his victory.

Hughes: He can't think of anything else to say but what I said to him.

GSP: The mistake I did was to say that in front of 5 million pay-per-view viewers and all the crowd in the arena.

Hughes: How many weeks later and I haven't even thought about it and he's still bringing it up, trying to defend himself. So it's pretty obvious I'm in his head.

GSP: I respect him, I respect his skill, I respect him as a man, but I'm not afraid of him.

Hughes: There are so many variables that are going to be different this time. We're both different fighters than when we fought last time.

GSP: When I fought Matt Hughes the first time, I remember that at the stare-downs [the traditional meeting of the fighters in the ring] I couldn't even look him in the eyes because I was too impressed. I was fighting my idol, I was fighting a guy that—for me—was impossible to beat.

Hughes: He made a mistake. It doesn't change anything.

Not only were GSP's words better chosen and more to the point, he seemed happy and confident. If anything, it was Hughes who appeared agitated.

* * *

The fight opened slowly. The first blow thrown—a sweeping left kick from GSP that missed—was almost 10 seconds in. The pair punched each other for a while, with little damage done. GSP missed a high kick. Hughes responded with a leg strike that seemed more to put him off balance than do any damage to GSP. GSP connected with his own low kick, with similar results.

The pair continued striking inconclusively until GSP landed a couple of hard punches about a minute in. Taking advantage of his superior reach and striking ability, GSP added a high kick that glanced off Hughes's face and another leg kick. Although the fight hadn't developed a rhythm yet and neither had even attempted a takedown, GSP looked like he was in charge.

Hughes landed a jab, which GSP repaid with a kick to the body and a punch to the face. There was another quick jab by Hughes.

GSP then missed a roundhouse, but immediately connected with a spinning kick. After Hughes recovered, he grinned and invited GSP to high-five him. GSP obliged, but did not smile.

Hughes rushed him, but GSP caught his arms and stepped back, taking away his momentum. Realizing he was now the one in danger, Hughes disentangled and stepped off. Back to striking, GSP appeared to land three punches and one kick for every one jab Hughes connected on. Almost two and a half minutes in, GSP landed a groin strike. It ended up slightly off target because Hughes immediately grabbed his crotch and fell to his hands and knees.

GSP kept his distance. Referee "Big John" McCarthy stepped in between them and allowed Hughes to get up. McCarthy walked him over to his corner to see if he was okay. He was. McCarthy ruled the contact inadvertent, so the fight was back on, with no points deducted.

GSP landed a similar kick. Again Hughes grabbed his crotch and went down to hands and knees. This time, GSP reacted differently. Instead of being concerned and apologetic, he was angry. Instead of looking at Hughes to make sure he was okay, he called out to McCarthy. This time McCarthy had to get GSP to keep his distance.

McCarthy escorted Hughes to his corner where Hughes went back down to his knees and writhed in pain. McCarthy then went over to GSP and told him: "Listen to me, listen to me, your foot is hitting here and it's sliding up, okay? It's not that you're intending to do it, I understand that, okay? But you've got to make this a clean fight, and not let it come up, okay? Do you understand?"

GSP said he did. There has since been a great deal of debate in the mixed martial arts community about those two kicks. Some have said that GSP was targeting Hughes with illegal kicks. They claim that GSP would risk disqualification from a title fight. Others say that Hughes was acting. Some claim that he was trying to get a psychological edge on GSP by showing him that he could get him disqualified if he felt like it, and he was using the fear of disqualification to take away one of GSP's more effective weapons. Others are of the opinion that he was attempting to sully GSP's reputation and have him considered a dirty fighter. Officially, though, GSP kicked Hughes in the thigh twice, and his ankle slipped both times. No foul.

After Hughes took some time to recover, they went back to striking. If Hughes's intention was to take the low inside kick out of GSP's arsenal, he failed. GSP went back to it. It didn't connect, but it showed Hughes that he wasn't afraid to use it.

With neither fighter finding an advantage and time running out, GSP landed a kick to the midsection and a Superman punch to the head. Hughes seemed woozy and went down to his hands and knees. GSP lunged in. Hughes flipped over onto his back and GSP landed on top of him, punching at his head. The horn to conclude Round One sounded, but few heard it over the roar of the crowd. Goldberg, who was not watching the clock, said he thought that McCarthy was stopping the fight, awarding GSP a TKO. But he hadn't won. Still, the round ended with GSP decisively in command of his former hero. He was no longer in awe of anyone.

Hughes came out punching in Round Two. GSP responded with a weak inside kick and a roundhouse that just missed. GSP approached, sent in a strike for Hughes's face, but missed. Hughes got under and put his arms around GSP's waist. GSP recognized what was happening, got an arm between Hughes's arm and his own body and lifted Hughes out of his advantageous position. In a clinch, Hughes delivered some knees before GSP separated.

GSP landed a quick combination to Hughes's face, then another inside leg kick, much lower than the two that sent Hughes down earlier. They traded some punches, then GSP kicked low again. And again. The second one caught Hughes preparing his own kick and took his legs out from under him. He hit the mat, but popped right back up again. They went back to boxing with GSP following Hughes jab for jab and Hughes using his knee to ward off low kicks.

But he was not prepared for a high kick. Just as Hughes was getting low for a takedown attempt, GSP unleashed a huge left roundhouse that landed on Hughes's right ear. He staggered and went down, landing on his left hip. He rolled onto his back as GSP pounced on him, raining punches down on his face. Then came the elbows. Hughes was helpless, not even able to get his arms up to block. McCarthy called the fight.

Instead on his usual backflip, GSP went down to his knees. He didn't need any time for it to sink in. He had won. He was world champion. The only thing that he had wanted, had worked for since he was a kid was now his. He had resoundingly dominated the only man ever to beat him. He was literally weeping. His team came in and tackled him with hugs.

After lying there stunned for a few moments, GSP walked over to Hughes, congratulated him and promised him a rematch.

*   *   *

After the fight, GSP was unable to stop smiling. "It's the best moment of my career so far," he said. "And I look forward to defending my title." When asked how this fight would affect his life, he replied: "Security, it's financial security . . . I come from not a very rich family, so now it's awesome. It's the best job in the world, and I want to do it for a long, long time."

And he did get some financial security for beating Hughes. And it stood far beyond the $58,000 the UFC paid him that night

(Hughes made $95,000 despite the loss). Just a few months later, Stephane Patry, who at the time was working as GSP's manager, announced that he had signed a six-fight deal with the UFC. As a privately owned company, the UFC was not required to disclose the details of the contract—the payouts mentioned in this book are the fighting fees and winning purses reported to state and provincial gaming commissions and do not reflect the total payment to each fighter in the form of bonuses—but the media at the time estimated that the value of the contract was in the low seven figures.

CHAPTER 8

Being world champion was the culmination of all of GSP's dreams, but he knew he had to defend the title to keep it. Besides former champs Matt Hughes and BJ Penn, there were plenty of guys out there who would give anything they had to get a shot at that belt.

GSP's first title defense would come on April 7, 2007, at Houston's cavernous Toyota Center, which is not just the home of the NBA's Rockets but a place that has hosted many different WWE events. The event was called *UFC 69: Shootout*, a reference to it being held in Texas.

His opponent would be a familiar one. As winner of the welterweight division on *The Ultimate Fighter 4*, Matt Serra had earned the right to a title shot. He said publicly that he had wanted to fight Hughes, a man he intensely hated, rather than GSP, whom he considered a friend.

Against either man, it would appear that Serra would be fighting way, way over his head. Hughes's record and repeated title defenses spoke for themselves. GSP was not only 13–1 as a professional, but he came back and destroyed the only man who had ever beaten him, and that was the tough Hughes. Besides, both of those men were brought into *The Ultimate Fighter 4* specifically to teach guys like Serra.

And Serra had a patchy record as a pro. He had accumulated a 9–4 record, and he had already lost to Karo Parisyan (who had lost to GSP), Din Thomas (who lost in the semifinals on *The Ultimate Fighter 4*), BJ Penn (who had recently lost to both GSP and Hughes) and Shonie Carter (who also lost in the semifinals on *The Ultimate Fighter 4*). And even in his win on *The Ultimate Fighter 4*—which was subtitled *The Comeback* because all the contestants were UFC veterans who had fallen on hard times—Serra had just narrowly slipped past Chris Lytle with a split decision in the final.

As befitting the character he had presented throughout his career, Serra played the challenge for laughs, but with an underlying fatalistic philosophy. "I can only hope he takes me lightly," he said. "If he does, he's going to be in for a long night."

GSP responded in kind. "People say 'you are going to beat him easy,' but I never take any opponent lightly," he said. "I'm not going to do it. Matt Serra is not an easy opponent. He is better than me at submissions. If I take him lightly, it's going to be a long night for me."

Serra defended his right to be there, and pointed out that anything could happen in the Octagon. "People say that if I don't get the fight on the ground, I'm going to get destroyed," Serra responded. "I'm not going to say it's not going to happen, but it doesn't happen. I never get destroyed. Everyone I fight, they know they've been in a fight." Then he relented and said what everyone was thinking, that he was fortunate just to be there. "A lot of guys go their whole careers without a title fight," he said with a smile. "And I have one."

Although GSP and opponent Matt Hughes were all smiles at the weigh-in for UFC 79, there was significant bad blood between the two. GSP would avenge his first-ever professional loss to Hughes at UFC 50 for a second time with a second-round submission at UFC 79.

UFC president Dana White plays to the Montreal crowd before UFC 83, the organization's first show in Canada, wearing a Canadiens jersey. The giant Bell Centre sold out in less than a minute.

At UFC 83 in Montreal, GSP won the undisputed UFC welterweight title in front of an appreciative hometown crowd. He also exacted revenge on one of only two men ever to beat him in the Octagon, Matt Serra, earning a TKO in the second round.

By the time GSP fought BJ Penn for a second time at UFC 94, he was not just champion but a recognized star in the sport with many lucrative sponsorships.

GSP beat former UFC lightweight and welterweight champion BJ Penn for a second time at UFC 94 in Las Vegas. GSP won by TKO when Penn received doctor's advice not to continue after the fourth round.

Late in their fight at UFC 111, GSP managed to get Dan Hardy in an armbar. Although that hold usually gives GSP a quick submission, Hardy managed to tough it out and make it to the end of a fight, losing by unanimous decision.

Heavily favored going into their fight at UFC 111, GSP was later criticized for methodically beating challenger Hardy instead of knocking him out or forcing him to submit.

A resourceful and ruthless strategist, GSP broke the orbital bone over Josh Koscheck's right eye early in their fight at UFC 124 and continued to work on it all night. Terribly battered, the challenger lost by unanimous decision.

When GSP beat Koscheck to retain his title at UFC 124, the hometown crowd went wild. The Montreal police had a riot control team in place just in case he lost.

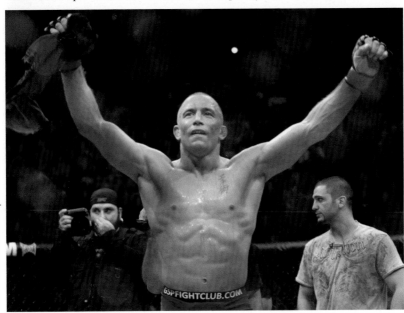

Everywhere he fights, GSP attracts a lot of Canadian fans. These women – (from left to right) Amy Coveney, Tonya Woroniuk, Meagan Minaker and Rachel Geurts – drove from Winnepeg to Minneapolis to watch GSP beat Jon Fitch at UFC 87.

GSP's daily training regime is shorter but more intense than that of other UFC fighters. He works on all aspects of the sport and can drop 15 pounds in just four days.

Because of his good looks, charm and wit, GSP has become a favorite among fans and corporate sponsors alike.

Analyst Joe Rogan said that the only thing GSP had to worry about was not taking Serra seriously. "There's gotta be a part of him that thinks this is an easy fight for him," he said.

Everybody had gotten on the GSP bandwagon. Bodog, one of the most prominent sports betting organizations, set the odds at GSP -950/Serra +800. That meant if you bet $1,000 on GSP and he won, you'd earn just $52.63 but if you bet $1,000 on Serra and he won, you'd get back $7,000 more than your initial stake. Performify, a respected online fight analysis site, agreed: "Frankly, Serra has no business being in the Octagon tomorrow against St-Pierre. I understand this fight was a condition of winning the welterweight class of *The Ultimate Fighter 4*. However, Serra has essentially no chance of making this fight remotely competitive, let alone winning it."

* * *

Just before the main event, there was another welterweight bout featuring a pair of hot up-and-comers. Albuquerque-native Diego "The Nightmare" Sanchez was considered a future champion and had amassed an incredible 17–0 record as a pro with wins over guys like Joe Riggs and Parisyan. His opponent was a trash-talking wrestler from western Pennsylvania named Josh "Kos" Koscheck, who had an 8–1 record with his only notable win coming against Pete Spratt.

Surprisingly, Sanchez was totally dominated. He didn't look like he should have even been in the same ring with Koscheck, who was chasing Sanchez around the Octagon when he wasn't hitting him. It was a unanimous 30–27 decision for Koscheck.

As usual for the main event, Serra, the challenger, entered first to polite applause. He showed his trademark sense of humor by choosing a remix of "Gonna Fly Now" (the theme from *Rocky*) as his entrance music. GSP came in with his now familiar "Samurai" by Parisian hip-hopper Shurik'n. The crowd was firmly behind GSP.

The two men were a study in fighter contrasts. GSP was much taller, with longer limbs and broader shoulders. He was thinner and sinewy. Serra, on the other hand, was short and thick with muscle. Even if you didn't know anything about mixed martial arts, it would be obvious that GSP would be better off striking, and Serra's best chance would be to get in close and grapple, taking away GSP's huge six-inch reach advantage. And that was the consensus among analysts—both paid and otherwise—before the fight. If Serra had even the remotest hope of winning, it would appear that he would have to do it on the ground.

To everyone's surprise, Serra came out punching. He quickly started serving up hard rights, then backing off. GSP delivered a head-high kick that missed, then connected on one to Serra's chest. GSP kicked again, and Serra blocked it. Serra sent in a low kick that hit GSP, but also gave him an opportunity to smash Serra's face with a hard left.

The two traded combinations, and Serra again ducked a high kick. After some dancing, Serra came in with some strong body blows. After GSP missed yet another kick, Serra went in, delivered a body shot and then a shin kick. After stepping away, he went back in for a low combination. Then he lunged in with some punches. It nearly became a clinch, but GSP threw him off.

Serra was doing a great job—not only ducking just about everything GSP threw at him, but also controlling the tempo of the fight. Then he moved in for a cross-and-hook combination that not only surprised GSP, but almost sent him to the mat. Taking a few steps to recover, GSP saw Serra coming at him and retreated toward the fence, slipping again on his way. With GSP standing and exposed, Serra delivered another left-right combination with the right cross sending GSP sideways, then down to the canvas on his knees. He grabbed Serra around the waist, literally to pull himself up, and Serra took advantage of his exposed face to land a quick flurry of small punches. GSP later described the punch that sent him down as hitting his carotid artery and said that he never really recovered from it during the fight.

Separated, Serra landed another quick combination, but this time it was the left that sent GSP down. Groggily, GSP righted himself and Serra rushed at him, striking repeated blows to his chest and belly. The momentum sent GSP backward, but he reversed it and went down on his knees, gripping Serra around his right calf. Serra pushed him off and hit him in the face again.

Hughes, ringside, knew something was wrong but couldn't believe it. "He's hurt," he later recalled. "Wait a minute. He can't be hurt. He's fighting Matt Serra."

As GSP was getting up slowly, Serra pounded him with yet another quick combination. It sent GSP down. He was on his back. Serra leaned in over him and started hammering him with terrifying power and brutality. GSP could do nothing but try to get his right arm in front of his face. Ref "Big John" McCarthy called it. TKO, Serra.

It was over. GSP was no longer champion. He had defended his title for just 3 minutes and 25 seconds. Less than five months after he took the belt from Hughes, he had to hand it to Serra.

Instead of GSP's backflip, the stunned crowd was treated to Serra's one-handed cartwheel.

* * *

The fight is still considered one of the biggest upsets in mixed martial arts history. Afterward, Serra explained that he had worked specifically on boxing because he knew it would be very difficult to bring GSP down and that nobody—especially not GSP himself—would have thought he'd come out striking.

GSP came out of the dressing room in a sharp black suit and silver tie. He looked somber and had bruises over quite a bit of his face. When asked what went wrong, he replied: "I was maybe too stiff. I tried to rush too much in the fight. I was . . . I don't know, I don't know. Some nights, it's not your night and that night was not my night. I have no excuse, I was in good shape. I was ready to do ten rounds. Just got caught with a punch, a right hook, and I was never able to come back. I don't know what to say. I've got to get back on top . . . and I'm ready for that challenge."

He then explained that the first stage after losing a fight was anger, but the eventual goal was acceptance of the fact. And only after that could he mount a comeback. Then he apologized to his fans.

*   *   *

If it was hard to accept the loss to Hughes, it was excruciating to accept the loss to Serra. Against Hughes he knew what his mistakes were, and how to correct them. But against Serra he was just plain outsmarted and outfought.

Eventually, GSP followed some advice from Vermont-based sports psychologist Brian Cain. Cain told him to carry a brick around with him everywhere he went to symbolize the emotional baggage he was carrying around after the loss. "You would never carry a brick all day and then go to the gym at nine o'clock at night and expect to have a good training session," Cain said. "You'd be physically exhausted. Well, psychologically, we do the same thing all the time. We carry what I'd call a mental brick when we don't let go of a loss, we don't let go of a problem, we don't let go of something someone said about us that we've got no control over. And if you hold on to that stuff, it wears on your mind, it wears on your heart and it's going to hold you back and tear you down, and make you exhausted just as it would if you were actually carrying a physical brick." GSP named the brick "Matt Serra."

After a few days, Cain told GSP to toss the brick away into the water so he would never see it again. So now it lies at the bottom of the St. Lawrence River. "It made me feel good. It made me feel very good, actually," GSP said later. "It looked dumb, but it made me feel very good."

But losing the title was hardly GSP's only problem. He revealed in an interview that his mind may have been elsewhere that night because a cousin of his—whom he described as more like a younger brother—had been in a coma after a car accident and later died. At about the same time, his father had taken gravely ill. He pointed out that those incidents left him only two weeks to train for the fight and that he was unprepared. He also alluded to a knee injury.

Serra was taken aback by those comments, considering them a dig by GSP, as though he was saying that if those things hadn't happened, he would have won easily. He answered those claims by giving a reporter a long and strangely entertaining tirade:

> Georges St-Pierre is a pathetic liar. He stood up after the fight like a man and admitted he got beat. Now this bullshit? How do you do a total 180? It's so disheartening. I earned this. I worked my friggin' ass off for this fight. All I did was give him respect and now he wants to save face by shitting on me? All I heard before the fight was how he was going to train like he never trained before and that he had to be absolutely perfect, and now he says he didn't train. So which is it? Are you a liar now or a liar

then? Everything is a cliché with this guy. Stop reading from the script for once and speak from the heart. Don't get me wrong, he's a good, talented fighter, but he got beat. I know it's hard for his camp to believe that Superman lost, but he did . . . Now we see what he's really made of. He was calling me his friend before the fight and now all of the sudden I was never anything more than an acquaintance. Well fuck you. I don't want to be your friend. Hit the road, Frenchy.

He had a point. GSP had actually told the same reporter—MMAMania's Jesse Holland—before the fight that he was training as hard as he ever had and was totally injury free. And there were persistent rumors that GSP was holidaying in France just weeks before the fight. Even his own entourage turned on him. "Let's just say he partied a little bit too much," said manager Stephane Patry.

GSP wanted to put it all behind him. "He can say whatever he wants, it's not going to get into my head," he replied through reporters. "I'm going to hit him as hard as I can either way." It was a thinly veiled request for a rematch.

*　*　*

And it was at this time that GSP changed again. Fans had already seen the remarkable growth in maturity from the giddy 21-year-old kid who beat Pete Spratt for a shot at the UFC to the calm, confident 25-year-old man who claimed the title from Matt Hughes. An athlete who trained alongside him at Tristar Gym told me that he saw a different man. "He was different. More serious, not sad or angry, but serious all the time. He came in; he worked, didn't talk and left. He was all about great, intense focus."

GSP changed out of necessity. And he started by breaking out of the cocoon of supporters and hangers-on who had helped him lose the straight and narrow path. "[The loss] taught me what it takes to become world champion," he recalled later. "And when I lost to Matt Serra, it taught me what it takes to stay world champion. You know when you become world champion at 25 years old and everybody around you—in the gym, everywhere—tell you how great you are and things like that, it makes you believe that you're in a box that separates you from the other fighters. But this box, this line is an illusion. And that's what happened. Even though I'm not a cocky guy, I got caught in those situations, many other things. I made many mistakes."

Previously, he had basically looked after his own training, hiring local coaches and traveling down to New York City to train with Renzo Gracie. But since Serra was far more entrenched in the Gracie camp, GSP abandoned it. Instead, like many athletes, he chose to train in Denver, where the thin atmosphere makes working out much more intense. Then he moved on to Albuquerque, where he trained with legendary coach Greg Jackson.

Jackson's family had a very athletic and powerful bloodline— his father, uncle and brother were all championship wrestlers. Like GSP, Jackson decided to learn martial arts at a young age for self-protection. As he grew older and more proficient, he began to mix wrestling with judo and came up with his own martial art, which he called gaidojutsu (basically "the way of the foreigner"). Introduced to mixed martial arts in much the same way GSP was, by watching a tape of *UFC 1*, he became interested in other forms of martial arts. He studied muay Thai under perennial champion Michael Winkeljohn, and the two developed a successful professional relationship that continues today.

Jackson's gym and system were renowned throughout the mixed martial arts world—Sherdog.com, a leading online mixed martial arts magazine, reported that Jackson-trained fighters held an amazing 81 percent winning record in the UFC. It was a wise and perhaps obvious choice to go there, but not an easy one for GSP. Until then, he had coaches and managers, of course, but they were Montrealers who answered to him. Going to Jackson meant giving up control and being one of many fighters who were training at the facility. It was like going to school, or more like going to boarding school because he had to break close ties with just about everything he had in professional life up to that point.

It was a bold strategic move, one that left more than a few Montreal-area friends feeling a little betrayed. One who understood was long-time trainer and friend Firas Zahabi, who was retained. "Georges is a very sweet nice guy, very down-to-earth," he said. "But you can't go to war with that mentality. When you go to war, you've got to be ready to put everything on the line and you've got to forget about being nice. He can do that."

It was a wise choice. GSP gained a great deal of strength, discipline and technique under Jackson's direction. GSP made another smart move at Jackson's compound, deciding to train with only bigger opponents—under the philosophy that if he practices against the big men, fighting against welterweights would seem relatively easy. He sparred frequently and came close with 205-pound light heavyweight contender (and future champ) Rashad "Suga" Evans and similarly sized Keith "The Dean of Mean" Jardine.

And, in perhaps the most meaningful move of his career, GSP changed managers. GSP needed someone who was as tough and prepared in the boardroom as he was in the Octagon. In an unprecedented move, he hired Shari Spencer in July 2007 after she showed him a presentation that he was impressed by. At a time when other fighters were represented by retired fighters, coaches or event organizers—Dana White himself had represented fighters before being named president of the UFC—GSP went not only with a woman, but one with no previous ties to the mixed martial arts world. Instead, she came from financial services management.

Almost 20 years earlier, Spencer and some friends founded a financial services firm called Accounts Recovery International in her native Georgia. On a website for medical professionals, the company's primary mandate was made clear in its sales pitch:

Accounts Recovery International, Inc. (ARI) offers professional bad debt recovery and extended business office services to hospitals and physicians that will enhance their current Revenue Cycle. Our staff is prepared to deliver such services as primary/secondary insurance billing and follow up, denial management, inhouse collections, and business office outsourcing as needed. Our goal is to provide exceptional customer service to our clients and their patients while bringing accounts to a positive resolution. No project is too big or too small. If you need assistance just call.

While collecting unpaid hospital bills will not make you many friends, it will most certainly hone your negotiating skills. While serving as the company's director, Spencer also attended and graduated from the prestigious Goizueta Business School at Atlanta's Emory University, a breeding ground for high-powered CEOs. She began to negotiate fights on GSP's behalf, groom his public image and—in another precedent-setting move—pursue sponsors outside the mixed martial arts world because, as she put it, GSP "appeals to women." One of her first acts was to take a PowerPoint presentation, complete with published numbers, to the notoriously blunt White to illustrate why her client deserved to be paid more.

There was more good news. GSP was able to track down a brain specialist who could treat his father. And GSP also worked hard to put the Serra loss and subsequent feud behind him. In an interview, he explained why he said what he did about the loss: "I felt like after my loss, I had so many people tell me 'how come you didn't look the same? You didn't look sharp, what happened to you?' and stuff like 'during your ring walk you didn't look like yourself' and stuff like that. So I felt like I had to explain myself and I made a mistake. I apologize though and now it's over . . . I'm a personal fighter with a lot of pride, and I shouldn't have said anything no matter what. If I took the fight it's because I'm ready to deal with the consequences, so if I lost I have to deal with that and take my loss like a man."

*   *   *

The road back to the top would start in Las Vegas. *UFC 74: Respect* was scheduled for the Mandalay Bay Events Center on August 25, 2007. The main event was a heavyweight bout between long-time champ Randy Couture and Brazilian challenger Gabriel "Napão" Gonzaga.

GSP's opponent would be Josh Koscheck. Considered a hot prospect since the Sanchez fight, Koscheck came from an outstanding wrestling background, making Division 1 All-American four times and becoming national champion in 2001. A smart kid, he earned a degree while wrestling and coaching at a high school in Erie, Pennsylvania, and the University of Buffalo before becoming a professional fighter. He participated in the first season of *The Ultimate Fighter* as a middleweight and showed his lack of experience in his first fight by forgetting to strike his downed opponent, Chris "The Crippler" Leben. The other fighters started calling him "carpet," because all he did was cover guys. He ended his tenure there by losing a split decision to Sanchez in the semifinal.

And *The Ultimate Fighter* showed that he was something of an individual. He dyed his dark, curly hair blond and was always helpful to the other fighters, but liked to drink and could get a bit mischievous.

But he had matured as a fighter. With a 9–1 professional record and a convincing win over Sanchez, Koscheck was undeniably a fighter on the rise.

In the official prefight interview, he came across as serious and respectful, at least at first. He described how much work he had done and how he had improved as a fighter, becoming a more complete package, rather than just a wrestler. He said positive things about GSP, even after the reporter tried to goad him into something more by pointing out that Serra had said that he felt sorry for whomever GSP's next fight was against. Koscheck deflected the barb, and spoke about how he hoped GSP and he would "put on a good show for the fans." Later, he changed tack and pointed out that GSP lacked "heart" and "a chin" and promised that if he could get the same shots in against him that he did against Sanchez, GSP "would be going to sleep."

The interview shows two very different Koschecks. Is the real one the guy who's polite until he talks long enough and gets confident enough to let out his inner braggart, or is he actually a respectful fighter to whom it occurred that he could get more hype (and presumably better fights and more money) if he said controversial things?

GSP, on the other hand, was his typical confident yet respectful self: "Well, he's a very good striker but I think I'm better than him at pretty much everything. I'm gonna have to dictate the pace and make him fight my fight, not his fight . . . he's got a great right hand, great guillotine, he's an awesome wrestler . . . The guy has everything, he's a top guy right now but I'm glad to fight him. I wanted to have the best opponent possible after my loss. I wanted to get back on track with everything, that's why I'm happy to fight him."

Confirming his reputation as a one-of-a-kind individual, Koscheck came out to a hip-hop song about himself, sung by himself, with many references to other UFC fighters. It's a testament to how popular GSP was even then that the Las Vegas crowd started booing Koscheck even before he appeared from the tunnel.

And, predictably, the cheering started as soon as the first strains of Rohff's "Dirty Hous" began to play—well before GSP actually appeared. In a direct contrast to his old style of entrance, bounding down the aisle high-fiving everyone who could reach him, GSP this time strode confidently, acknowledging only a few people he knew. Rogan pointed out that he looked more focused, not like he did against Serra. Although Koscheck was three years older than the 26-year-old GSP, he looked like the classic young upstart going up against a proven veteran.

Koscheck opened up with a combination, but didn't connect. He finally did get a hard right in, but GSP shrugged it off. GSP missed a kick. Koscheck hit with a kick low, but it left him off balance and GSP dove in for a classic shoot.

Koscheck was on his back with GSP on top. GSP lifted him slightly and repositioned him away from the fence while getting a couple of quick headshots in. Koscheck got onto his left side, but that allowed GSP to get one hand behind his knees and the other behind his neck, reducing his guard to half. GSP got a couple of nice head and then smaller body shots in.

Koscheck finally managed to stand them both up by grabbing hold of GSP's left leg. GSP sprawled to prevent a takedown, but Koscheck was persistent, lifting the leg and forcing him to hop on the other. Koscheck was reaching with his left hand for GSP's other leg, and just when it seemed GSP would free himself, Koscheck pushed hard, grabbed the leg and took GSP to the ground.

With Koscheck on top and GSP in butterfly guard, both men tried to isolate an arm. When that didn't work, it was apparent GSP was going for a triangle. Koscheck saw it and prevented it. GSP tried to get both men up, but it only allowed Koscheck to land a nasty right to his face. The horn sounded to end the round.

Although GSP had spent more time in control, Koscheck ended the round that way. It could have gone either way.

Round Two began with GSP faking a big kick, then landing a glancing one off Koscheck's thigh. He then landed a jab-kick combination. As Koscheck was recovering, GSP shot in for a takedown attempt. He couldn't just knock him down as his back was against the fence, so GSP lifted his thigh and spun him around onto his back.

Koscheck was in half guard, and still GSP tried to isolate his right arm for a kimura. As GSP extended his arm, Koscheck slipped it out of his grasp and put it under his chin. GSP isolated the right arm again. Koscheck slipped out, but GSP had gained side control, a much better position for applying a kimura.

Koscheck managed to roll and get up a little, but GSP threw him back down again. Koscheck managed to establish full guard, and GSP could do little but send a few punches in at his face. The crowd was chanting "GSP! GSP!" while the former champ was attempting to get side control, but Koscheck tied up his legs with his own.

Koscheck then turned onto his side. With both men's arms intertwined, GSP put one knee in front of Koscheck's face and the other foot behind his neck. It was an effective move to cut short any escape plans, and looked very much like he was sitting on his head. Then GSP put all of his efforts into separating Koscheck's arm from its protected position and stretching it into a kimura. But Koscheck held out until the horn.

The first round may have been a toss-up, but the second was obviously GSP's.

GSP began the third round on the offensive, landing a few low leg kicks. Koscheck answered with a high combination and landed another punch when GSP missed a kick. The two sparred about evenly, then Koscheck went in for a body combination and got rewarded with a nice uppercut. GSP low kicked him again, then sent in a high kick that grazed Koscheck's face. Then GSP landed a number of unanswered punches and kicks. Koscheck went in with a wide right and slipped, but took advantage by grabbing GSP's thigh. Once again, he drove him back almost to the fence, hopping all the way.

It was a stalemate for some time, but finally Koscheck drove GSP across the blood-stained canvas. It looked good for him until he slipped. In a flash, Koscheck was on his back with GSP on top of him again. Koscheck had full guard, so GSP went into the old ground-and-pound routine. Facing a steady stream of elbows, Koscheck began to look worried. With less than a minute to go, Koscheck made a desperate attempt at an arm bar.

With 10 seconds left, the crowd began to cheer loudly. Koscheck made one last attempt to save himself with a flurry of wild punches, but got beaten back down. Just before the horn, GSP leapt off of Koscheck and was working him into a leg lock.

The horn sounded. GSP got up and mimed putting a belt on. He wanted his title shot. He hugged and spoke with Koscheck, then hugged and thanked his new cornerman, Jackson. Again the crowd was chanting "GSP! GSP!" It was a unanimous decision. Two of the three judges thought Koscheck won the first round, while the other believed GSP won all three.

After the decision was announced, GSP embraced Koscheck and told him "you're gonna be back" before Rogan grabbed him. Asked if it was a big win, GSP told him it was huge. "I've come such a long way, it's like I was reborn just now," he said. "I want to apologize to my fans for my last fight [but] I think it's the best thing ever to happen to me for my career, and now I'm a brand-new version. I'm better than ever." Rogan was wrapping up the interview when GSP told him he wasn't finished and asked for the microphone. Then he challenged his own organization: "I have a message for Dana White and Mr. Fertitta. Alright, they like to have a show. I gave a good show tonight, and I want to do something. So far, the UFC has been great. The crowds have been unbelievable. They have been everywhere, in Las Vegas, in California and England. But if they come to Montreal, my people will go crazy. And it would give them a show like they have never seen before."

White smiled amicably and clapped while the crowd around him roared its approval for the UFC to visit another city that, apparently, they thought had earned the right.

And things were looking up for GSP financially as well. His payout for *UFC 69* was $140,000. It was still dwarfed by Couture's $250,000, but represented a huge leap forward for him and for welterweights, who were traditionally paid much less than heavyweights. Koscheck, for example, made just $10,000.

* * *

In fact, the welterweight division was the one to watch for most fans. It was rife with drama. There was bad blood between Hughes and Serra, Hughes and GSP, and GSP and Serra, and all three had held the championship belt in a span of less than five months. Another former champion, Penn, could not be counted out. Chris Lytle could be dangerous and so could Koscheck with a little refinement. And new threats were emerging. Jon Fitch was another college wrestling star. He beat Sanchez at *UFC 76* to go 17–2 with one no contest and a 15-match undefeated streak. And Brazilian Thiago "Pitbull" Alves was also deemed by many as a potential future champion because of his often dominating performances against quality fighters.

Recognizing this, the UFC retooled *The Ultimate Fighter* for its sixth season. They dropped the series number for a more exciting subtitle; it became *The Ultimate Fighter: Team Hughes vs. Team Serra*. In it, 16 fighters—all welterweights—were pitted against each other on two teams, one coached by Hughes, the other by Serra. All of this, of course, would be a prelude to the Hughes-Serra title fight at *UFC 79: Nemesis*.

There weren't as many fireworks between the coaches as many predicted, but it was an entertaining series. One competitor, Roman Mitichyan, broke his elbow in the first episode and was replaced by Jon "War Machine" Koppenhaver. Although Serra's fighters won six of the first eight fights, the final featured two of Hughes's guys—Mac Danzig and Tommy Speer.

Danzig dominated Speer, applying a rear-naked choke just 2:01 into the first round. But there was no $100,000 contract or $100,000 endorsement deal like Serra was given. Instead, he was paid $16,000 for the fight and promised another. Danzig then announced that he had only fought as a welterweight to get on the show and that he was going to drop to his more natural lightweight division.

*   *   *

The stage was then set for the fight the mixed martial arts world was dying to see: Serra against Hughes. Even though there was a light heavyweight bout with two of the sport's biggest stars—Chuck

Liddell and Wanderlei "The Axe Murderer" Silva—the welter-weight match was to be the mainest of main events.

Just before American Thanksgiving—the fight was set for December 29, 2009—Serra was training and being filmed for a prefight promotional video. He was demonstrating something to his partner when he heard a click and felt a searing pain. "I've never been stunned by a stun gun before, but that's kind of what it felt like, I guess." His students helped him up and to the shower. His brother arrived and had to put his socks and shoes on for him.

At a Long Island hospital the next day, Serra was diagnosed with two herniated discs in his lower back. Stubbornly, he waited a couple of days before informing the UFC that he was in too much pain to fight. "This is the hardest thing I've ever had to do," the champ told a reporter at MMANews. "I've never had a back injury before; I could hardly get off of the MRI table. There is no way I can train through this, and I'm devastated, especially because this was such an important fight. I was looking forward to fighting Matt Hughes. All my training was going phenomenally until Monday. All I can do now is to get better and to fight again as soon as possible."

With Serra sidelined, the UFC and the welterweight division had to move on without him. White picked GSP to fight Hughes for the interim welterweight title with the understanding that the winner would be champion only until Serra was back in fighting shape and then would be required to fight Serra for the title. Kindly, White told Serra before anyone else, and the champ was cool with the measure. When asked what he thought about the match, he was his usual frank self. "I almost don't want to say anything because chances are GSP's going to beat his ass again, like worse than the first time," Serra said. "And I'm fighting GSP and not him. I'd rather fight Matt for more than one reason."

Although he didn't think he was going to be fighting for a while yet, GSP was not only willing to take the fight, but was in shape for it. "I feel privileged to have this fight and I wish nobody bad luck, but Serra got hurt and I'm able to step in," he said. "I'm already in unbelievable shape and I decided that it would be worth it to step up and take this shot."

Of course he would. He had to. This new GSP—confident as champion, tempered by bitter defeat, and better trained and in better shape than at any other time in his career—knew he was the best welterweight fighter in the world. And the best in the world would never turn down a title fight, interim or not.

CHAPTER 9

In the period between losing to Matt Serra and beating Josh Koscheck, GSP had effectively become a different person. And a better fighter. By focusing and enrolling in Greg Jackson's school, he was preparing to achieve his one true goal.

For better or worse, Matt Hughes took the opposite tack. For many years, Hughes had trained under the Miletich Fighting System. Founded in 1997 by the UFC's first-ever lightweight champion, Pat Miletich (back then, lightweight meant anyone under 200 pounds), the Bettendorf, Iowa, school was one of the first dedicated mixed martial arts facilities outside Brazil and featured championship-level fighters such as Tim Sylvia, Jens "Little Evil" Pulver, Robbie Lawler, Jeremy "Gumby" Horn and Hughes himself. In fact, Hughes had been training there since the end of 2000.

But in the autumn of 2007, Hughes, Lawler, boxing coach Matt Pena and wrestling coach Marc Fiore (Hughes's long-time cornerman) left Miletich's organization to form their own gym, Team Hughes. While the others were involved to some degree, the fact that it was called Team Hughes accurately indicated who was making the major decisions. Training took place in a facility called the H.I.T. (for Hughes Intensive Training) Squad in Granite City, Illinois, an atavistic town of 31,000 just across the Mississippi from Iowa.

At the time, Hughes and his team said the split with Miletich was totally amicable and stemmed from Hughes's desire to be near his family (Hillsboro is about an hour's drive from Granite City) and because his involvement in coaching on *The Ultimate Fighter* made him realize that he loved to teach. Some insiders said that although the Miletich camp was not saying anything, they were angry not just at the loss of revenue, but also at what seemed like a personal betrayal. Many observers at the time speculated that Hughes was setting himself up with a franchisable business for a new career after he stopped fighting professionally.

*   *   *

The interim title fight was a marketing manager's dream. Hughes was the most dominant welterweight—and arguably the most dominant fighter—in UFC history. He had successfully defended his title seven times (it could have been eight times had Riggs made his weight) and had destroyed the legendary Royce Gracie. GSP, on the other hand, was considered the most naturally talented welterweight ever to walk the canvas and the future of the entire sport, not only his weight division. Hughes had beaten GSP. GSP had beaten Hughes. The two men had very different personalities, and both had huge dedicated fan bases that were often at odds with each other. Neither fighter liked the other one personally, although GSP continued to say polite things about Hughes.

UFC President Dana White pushed every angle he could. "Obviously, the loss of Matt Serra was brutal, but the great thing about the UFC is that we can put together great fights like Hughes/

St-Pierre at a moment's notice and bounce right back," he said at a press conference. "I have the utmost respect for both Hughes and St-Pierre for stepping up for this fight, and not only are the fans going to see two of the greatest welterweights of all-time settle their score in a rubber match, but [they're] going to do it in a five-round interim title fight, and the winner is going to face off next year against Matt Serra for the undisputed title."

Despite the hype machine, the normally outspoken Hughes was reserved for this one, pointing out what an important fight it was to both of them and how he knew that every fight with GSP was a "war." While he praised GSP, he couldn't resist a dig at the sidelined champ. "If there's someone I want to fight out there it's St-Pierre," he said. "Because he's at the top. . . . This is definitely a tougher fight than Matt Serra. Georges St-Pierre just brings so many more tools into the Octagon than Matt Serra." Many fans responded to this kinder, gentler Hughes by filling online forums with posts declaring him in decline at age 34 and without the necessary aggression to be the great fighter he was before.

For his part, Serra responded predictably. "I can't believe the position this puts me in," he said. "I'm actually rooting for Matt Hughes, so I can beat his ass."

And GSP answered the question he knew was on everybody's mind. "I have no doubt I'm going to win that fight," he said. "I'm going with a very good mental state this time. I will come well prepared. I will come with a game plan."

Despite being a last-minute replacement, GSP was favored to win by oddsmakers. The most commonly given odds put GSP at -240 and Hughes at +190, meaning a winning $1,000 bet on GSP would return $417, while the same bet on a victorious Hughes would return $1,900.

The hype paid off. Although some of the fans were there for the Chuck Liddell–Wanderlei Silva light heavyweight undercard, the interest in *UFC 79* was huge. The capacity of the Mandalay Bay venue limited the live crowd to just 11,075, but they paid a total of $4,994,000 for their tickets (a $451 average), as opposed to the $2,100,000 that 14,701 fans paid to attend *UFC 78* (a $143 average) in Newark six weeks earlier. Additionally, the pay-per-view audience of more than 700,000 positively dwarfed the 400,000 or so who subscribed to *UFC 78*.

GSP looked laser sharp and intense as he calmly strode down to the Octagon. He entrance music was provided by Montreal hip-hoppers Sans Pression (their name means "without pressure" in French). The song "Territoire Hostile" is a cautionary tale about violence on the streets of Montreal. It wasn't for all tastes, but it was an excellent contrast to Hughes's trademark song "A Country Boy Can Survive."

The fight started slowly. The two men seemed to be sizing each other up, even though they had fought twice before. After about 15 seconds, Hughes went in for an unconventional takedown attempt, but missed. GSP dove in with fists flying after landing a kick to Hughes's chest. Hughes ducked and grabbed GSP around the hips to take him down. GSP spread his powerful legs, breaking Hughes's grip, and managed to straighten both men back up.

In a clinch, the men traded knees as Hughes groped for a thigh. But it was GSP, managing to get his right hand behind Hughes's left knee, who established control of the situation and pushed forward for the takedown. But Hughes immediately set up guard and started striking GSP in the head with his elbows. GSP replied with some quick, short punches. He pushed Hughes up against the fence to effect the ground-and-pound.

Hughes managed to lock his arms around GSP's torso. GSP slammed him against the canvas repeatedly. The round ended with GSP on top, landing punch after punch.

In the time between the rounds, Jackson instructed GSP while Horn appealed to Hughes to keep aware of GSP's left. The crowd couldn't stop. They were chanting "GSP! GSP! GSP!" Hughes didn't look like he did when he won fights. He looked nervous. GSP had a huge gob of petroleum jelly stuck above his right eyebrow. His cornermen should have wiped it off. They didn't.

GSP looked confident at the start of Round Two, delivering a high kick that Hughes had to block with his hands. After a few feints, the two got into a clinch. GSP threw Hughes backward to the canvas. The Las Vegas crowd was chanting "GSP! GSP!" again. GSP eventually achieved side control. Then he passed guard, getting seated upon Hughes's gut. Hughes managed to roll over, but GSP rode him and pulled him back down again. He was trying to set up a rear-naked choke, but had to content himself with a few punches to Hughes's face.

Hughes kept working and managed to get loose from GSP's grip and grasp GSP's thighs, but GSP pressed forward, took Hughes's left thigh in his hands and backed him up against the fence. Hughes spun out of GSP's grip and turned the tables, getting GSP's legs in his grasp. But he couldn't take him down. GSP kept widening his sprawl. No matter how hard Hughes worked, GSP was not going down. He grabbed a thigh, attempting to lift GSP off the canvas. It didn't happen. Back standing, the men traded knees before GSP slammed Hughes to the mat.

Hughes was on his back and passed his guard. GSP was on top. He tried a triangle choke, but backed off. He next tried a north-south position, and then concentrated on Hughes's right arm. Using both of his own arms, GSP managed to pry Hughes's right away from his body. Then he dropped back, pulled the arm and bent it backward. Hughes struggled, he panicked, he was in extreme pain. He submitted.

It was over. GSP beat Hughes the same way Hughes had beaten him. Never again would Hughes be able to joke about GSP needing to learn how to "defend the arm bar." It was best two out of three.

GSP was interim welterweight champion. After a quick breakdance celebration, he started pantomiming putting the belt around his waist. But when he was presented the interim title belt, he didn't put it on, instead handing it to a cornerman. He said that Matt Serra was the champion and that until he beat him he would not consider himself a champion.

He earned a belt that night—just not the one he really wanted.

* * *

GSP may not have liked the interim belt, but there were other benefits from fighting Hughes. GSP's pay packet had moved way upmarket. His official take home from *UFC 79* was $210,000. He was paid $80,000 for fighting, another $80,000 for winning and a further $50,000 bonus for "Submission of the Night." And he got his shot against Serra on what would become the biggest night of his life.

* * *

For decades the people in and around Montreal were immensely dedicated to their hockey team. For much of the twentieth century, the Montréal Canadiens, better known as the Habs, had a dominant streak that only baseball's New York Yankees could rival. They were the biggest show in town, and their home, the Montreal Forum, was sold out for every game and considered to be sacred ground by hockey fans everywhere.

But times changed. The league expanded, interest in hockey south of the border increased and players from Europe started coming across the Atlantic to play in North America. Canadians now accounted for about half of the NHL players and French-Canadians were a minority among them. The league instituted an entry draft. In that leveled playing field, the Habs fell from dominance.

In March 1996, the Habs left the Forum for a bigger, more modern arena called the Molson Centre. It was named after the brewery that owned the team. By that time, the look of the team had changed. Although management still made an effort to draft and acquire French-Canadian players, of the 40 players who took to the ice for the Habs that season, just 14 of them had roots in Quebec. And they traded away their best known French-Canadian player—goaltender Patrick Roy—to Colorado after he got into a fistfight with a coach who made fun of his poor English skills.

By 2008, the Bell Centre (Molson gave up the arena's naming rights to the Montreal-based communications giant after selling the team) was still selling out, but the days of Guy Lafleur, Jean Béliveau, Henri Richard and Maurice Richard were a distant memory. By that season, the Habs had lost a significant amount of their mystique and their connection with French-Canadians. Their captain was a plucky Finn, their leading scorer was an outgoing Russian, their best defender (and assistant captain) was a hulking Long Islander and their goalie was from a small town in British Columbia and couldn't speak a word of French. Perhaps even more significantly, they had not won a title since moving into the building.

In fact, many Montreal-area sports fans had a new idol who did his work on blood-stained canvas, not ice. GSP was a big star to mixed martial arts fans everywhere, but he was absolutely immense in Montreal. Bars that picked up the satellite feeds of his fights were packed and thunderous, turning people away as they reached capacity. Bell—which handled the UFC pay-per-view broadcasts in Canada—recorded bigger numbers when he fought than with any other broadcast. "A few years ago, Georges could walk down the street and nobody would bother him, nobody would even recognize him," said head trainer and friend Firas Zahabi, who has been with the team since 2001. "But now when he walks around or we go for lunch, he's always asked for autographs, he's always being mobbed."

"It happened really fast, everything, you know," said childhood friend Gerardo Lanctôt. "In four years he went from almost nothing to a big star."

His new boxing coach, Howard Grant (a Montreal-born former lightweight who retired with a 16-2 professional record), said he wasn't surprised. "The sky's the limit for Georges," he said. "The guy's popular, he's good-looking, he's charismatic."

Those facts did not escape Dana White. Not only did he bring the UFC to Canada for the first time, but he set up the GSP-Serra welterweight title fight in what amounted to the challenger's hometown. *UFC 83: Serra vs. St-Pierre 2* was set for April 19, 2008, at the Bell Centre.

White predicted—as GSP had earlier—that the UFC would have a great reception in Canada. "It's insane how big this sport is in Canada, and especially how many Canadians come down here, whether Georges St-Pierre is fighting or not," White said. "The sport is so big in Canada, it's mind-boggling to me."

And he was right. While most UFC events at the time had full houses only after hundreds or even thousands of free tickets were handed out, that wasn't the case in Montreal. After the reserved tickets were distributed, the remaining seats went on sale to the public. They sold out in minutes.

White was surprised and jubilant. "I'm excited to say that this event is a sellout, and the fastest one in UFC history," he said. "So it's safe to say we definitely will be back in Canada after this inaugural event."

Along with GSP, six other Canadian fighters—lightweights Sam "Hands of Stone" Stout and Mark Bocek as well as middleweights Jason "The Athlete" MacDonald, Joe "El Dirte" Doerksen, Jason "Dooms" Day and Kalib Starnes—were on the card. GSP's friend, middleweight Patrick Côté, was originally scheduled to fight American Alan "The Talent" Belcher, but suffered a sprained knee after slipping and falling on ice outside his home. Day took his place.

*   *   *

Clearly, the GSP who would be taking on Serra this time was not the same guy who had fought him a year earlier. His new training regimen was paying spectacular returns. "When we tested him originally, right after [the] Serra [fight], he had trouble with ten body-weight chin-ups," said new strength and conditioning coach Jonathan Chaimberg, owner of Montreal-base Adrenaline Performance Center fitness facilities. "And now, he's doing it with 100-pound dumbbells for three reps [of ten]."

He was stronger mentally and emotionally as well. GSP's father was recovering from a brain illness, thanks to the specialist GSP had found, which took a lot of stress off his shoulders. And, as he had when he lost to Hughes, he seemed to have learned from his mistakes against Serra. "The first time I fought Serra, he had the element of surprise, and he caught me right in the [right] spot with the right timing," he said. "Everything went so well for him, I tried to come back, I lost my equilibrium. I lost."

As usual, Serra did not keep his personality under wraps. When asked one word to describe GSP, he chose "tough." When asked one to describe Hughes, he said "dead"—although many fans insist that if you listen closely to the answer, he actually said "dick."

But it wasn't all fun and games. Despite being the champion, Serra was the oddsmakers' underdog. He wasn't the 10–1 long shot he was when he met GSP at *UFC 69*, but the line—GSP -450/Serra +350—was a metaphorical slap in the face to the champ. Serra got a little more serious and was trying to play it as though it was not a big deal for him. "The first time I fought him, it was kind of like *Rocky*—the guy that shouldn't even be in there with him, there's no way he's going to win—and it goes well," he said. "I love it when the people doubt me, I mean it's just, hey, it don't mean too much to me, man; it's all hype, it really is. It really boils down to two guys in a cage. No matter what people say—the so-called experts, the popular opinion, the critics—it don't mean anything to me, because I'm the guy in there. They're not in there fighting it for me. I'm in there. Am I going to get my ass beat? I don't know, we'll see." Not the most confident speech a champ has ever made.

As far as the event being in Montreal went, Serra knew he was going into hostile territory. "I'm expecting a lot of boos," he said, laughing. "It's all right, man, I've got thick skin, I'm a fighter. I look at it like there's no pressure on me. People are going to say, 'What if you lose the belt?' Dude, you're looking at the guy who wasn't even supposed to board the plane to get the belt."

GSP also acknowledged his home-field advantage. "[It's] the best scenario I could wish for," he said. "I'm fighting Matt Serra, the guy who beat me last time. I'm having my revenge. Plus, it's like I'm fighting in my backyard, in Montreal. In front of my people. And I'm fighting for a world title, so I couldn't wish for a better scenario than this."

Hughes also had to get his two cents in. He said he was "rooting" for GSP and would have gone to Montreal to see the fight, but had obligations at home and was going to watch it from his living room couch instead. "If GSP wins and Matt Serra loses, I've already asked the UFC if I could fight Serra," he told a reporter. "I just think him and I have some unfinished business so to speak with the reality show [*The Ultimate Fighter*]. And if Serra happens to pull out a victory, then I'll just go and I'll find somebody else to fight. I don't know who it'd be right now, but we'll just see."

* * *

The weigh-in was packed and tense. Before the fighters came out, the organizers showed videos of both GSP and Serra fighting and then claiming each had disrespected the other after their first fight. The crowd was chanting "GSP! GSP!" even before the challenger came out, and it went into full scream mode by the time he approached the risers. He took his jeans and T-shirt off, made weight and gave the crowd double okay signs. Once he stepped off the scale, drank deeply from a water bottle and started to get his jeans on, the crowd changed. The boos started once it was Serra's turn. He grinned and mocked the crowd with a peace sign. Someone shouted "Go back to Jersey, you bum!" As he stepped on the scale, the GSP! chant started again. The champ made weight and then posed for photographers with GSP for the old square-up shot. Both fighters said a few words, but it was almost too loud to hear them. GSP said fighting in the Bell Centre for a title would be "the best moment of my career." Serra made a joke about keeping his car running so he could make a hasty exit, win or lose.

The city was alive the night of the fight. There were 11 bouts that night, but everyone was there to see the main event. Of the other Canadians, Goulet, MacDonald and, surprisingly, Day, the last-minute replacement and underdog, won. Stout, Doerksen, Bocek and Starnes lost. In fact, Starnes looked so over his head and was so clearly outmatched against Nate "Rock" Quarry that the partisan pro-Canadian crowd booed him lustily and cheered when Quarry, an American, performed a mocking "Running Man" dance. Starnes survived the match, but it was the most lopsided decision in UFC history. And Starnes's contract with the UFC was cut two days later.

The entire card may as well have been a preamble because the crowd went wild as soon as they heard San Pression shout out "I'm back! I'm back!" It was GSP's latest entrance music, the Québécois hip-hop artist's song "Numéro 1." The lights were blinding. Everyone was standing. Every smartphone was recording video. Everyone else was taking pictures. And they were all screaming for Montreal's new hometown sports hero.

A fan jumped down to the fighters' level, but security wrestled him down and dragged him away.

Then darkness. And relative silence. Until the boos began to crescendo. Then the sounds of "Gonna Fly Now" mashed up with Memphis Bleek's "Like That" announced the champ was coming out.

The fighters usually size each other up for 10 to 15 seconds. There was none of that for this fight. Immediately Serra went in low, attempting a takedown, but GSP sprawled and got his arms around his torso. With one explosive jolt from his legs, he had Serra on his back. They were less than four seconds into the 25-minute scheduled bout.

Serra, a great BJJ technician after all his years with the Gracies, pulled guard and maintained half guard and the two were striking and grappling on the ground. If their first fight was a reversal of conventional wisdom, with Serra dominating a stand-up battle, this was a reversal of that reversal, with GSP putting the champ on the canvas right away. Analyst Joe Rogan admitted he was surprised. Again. Serra trapped GSP's left leg with his own, but GSP snapped out of it. The GSP! GSP! chant swelled with volume.

GSP started up some ground-and-pound. He got a few shots in, but so did Serra. They traded elbows. GSP rose and landed a huge combination to Serra's face. Then another. Serra was flailing. He was struggling, trying to get off his back. GSP looked far stronger, especially in his upper body, than he had in previous bouts. Another big elbow from GSP landed on Serra's face. Serra failed in a sweep attempt. It allowed GSP to pass Serra's guard and get into a side mount. Serra rolled onto his belly, a better defensive position, but one that took away any offensive potential. GSP hammered his head with his fist. Serra got up to his knees, but GSP twice pulled him back down.

Serra finally managed to stand with the help of the fence, but it cost him a knee to the gut. Having broken free, Serra did not look sure of his footing. He went in jabbing. He landed a couple of shots to the body before GSP sent in a Superman punch. Serra went back in jabbing, but GSP got in low, grabbed Serra's waist and threw him to the ground again. When the horn sounded, Serra was curled in a ball with GSP hammering away at him.

It was a dominating round. The champ was powerless as the challenger dictated every move and threw him to the ground like he was not even being opposed. The crowd was on its feet.

Round Two started with Serra jabbing. He threw a low outside kick at GSP's thigh. GSP grabbed Serra's leg and marched him through the Octagon and put him on his back again. Using the fence to get back up, the champ was thrown down again. Serra managed to get on his hands and feet, but could do little but try to protect his head. He managed to get up and out, but GSP again gave him a knee to the midsection to remember it by. GSP then grabbed his leg again, but this time Serra managed to hop out of the takedown attempt.

Back on his feet, Serra threw in his best weapon—the overhead right—but it just glanced off GSP. After a few jabs, Serra landed a head kick. GSP shook it off. He repaid the gesture with a spinning back kick that grazed Serra's chin. He went in low, GSP got lower, but Serra punched his way out of the takedown attempt. GSP used his reach advantage to land two quick jabs. Serra pulled back. His feet were heavy, he was leaning forward, he was dropping his hands. GSP landed three more jabs to Serra's face, then rushed in and took him down yet again.

With his forearm on Serra's throat to control Serra's head movement, GSP kept punching. As GSP started to work his legs with small kicks and knees, Serra got on his hands and knees. GSP kept punching. Serra slipped onto his back. As Serra struggled on the ground, GSP landed a huge left hook. Then a combination. With Serra back on his hands and knees, GSP held him and threw a few knee kicks to his body. Serra suddenly spun over on his back. GSP dove in, regained control and started slamming him again. Passing half guard, he achieved a side mount. Serra was back on his hands and knees. Again, GSP started sending in the knees. When it became clear Serra could do nothing but absorb GSP's blows, referee Yves Lavigne rushed in and separated the men.

He called it. TKO GSP. GSP was world champion once again, and he did it in front of "his people." They did their best to return the favor by screaming as loudly as they could. He did his celebratory backflip.

The jubilant crowd stayed cheering for a very long time before spilling into the streets of Montreal, where they were just as loud. When asked what he thought of Montreal, White couldn't hide his delight. "This is a hotbed for mixed martial arts now—obviously not only for the talent—but just so many fans here," he said. "The energy here tonight was more powerful than anywhere I've ever been. We did 21,390 people here—officially the biggest UFC event ever. I'd be back here every weekend, if we could."

Mixed martial arts had arrived as a major sport in Montreal. In Canada. And the one who had brought it there was a young man from Saint Isidore. In the ring, he looked nearly invincible. In front of the cameras, he was handsome, well-spoken, confident and even charming. He was a genuine star. And he was champion of the world.

CHAPTER 10

It was good to be champion again. But this was a different champion. Long gone was the young man who once admitted an addiction to visiting McDonald's for "two cheeseburgers and French fries." While he would occasionally visit a nice restaurant—like Montreal's 40 Westt Steakhouse or Panevino Ristorante in Las Vegas—to treat himself, the days of sodium- and fat-laden fast-food were over.

He would have to drive (or be driven) to either of those restaurants in a vehicle with tinted windows because he could no longer walk the streets of either city without being mobbed by adoring fans. "After I won the title [in Montreal], things just exploded," he said. "It was like that movie, *Dawn of the Dead*, with the zombies. I couldn't go anywhere."

Friends were concerned that he could be overextending himself. "He's an extremely generous guy, he has trouble saying 'no.' And now GSP is this big machine," said his old friend and early sparring partner Rudolphe Beaulieu. "The world asks for a lot more than it gives back to him."

But this more mature GSP had his own priorities. Quebec is a jurisdiction that does not require organizers of athletic contests to publish what they pay participants, so GSP's payoff for *UFC 83* has never been publicly disclosed. Educated estimates have placed it in the $200,000 to $250,000 range, even without bonuses. He later paid off his parents' mortgage on the house in Saint Isidore. He bought himself a nice, but hardly ostentatious, house in Candiac, a quiet South Shore suburb just east of Saint Isidore. He leased a luxury SUV big and powerful enough to handle Quebec winters. He lived—relatively speaking—large.

He was a different man in front of the cameras as well. He had gone from being the future of the UFC to the face of the UFC. The mainstream media—from ESPN to the *New York Times*—that had ignored the UFC and mixed martial arts for years now competed with one another to get a piece of his time. And he rewarded them with great interviews. He was handsome and impeccably dressed. Always an intelligent young man, GSP now spoke English with enviable fluency. He promoted mixed martial arts as a noble sport that was enjoyed by the original Olympians. Interviewers would sometimes have to get him back on subject when he started to talk about prehistoric biology or the views of nineteenth-century philosophers, a sign of his diverse reading interests. And he also had a fun-loving, even self-deprecating side. As Dana White said, "What's not to like about Georges St-Pierre?"

Indeed, he was a perfect spokesman for the UFC, and his new manager, Shari Spencer, saw that he could be far more than that. Many UFC fighters had sponsorship deals, and GSP was already among the better compensated. While the league had all kinds of major sponsors, like Harley-Davidson, for the most part the only sponsors the fighters had were companies directly related to mixed martial arts—supplements, equipment manufacturers, gyms and that sort of thing. Before he signed with Spencer, GSP was one of several fighters whose face would appear on 24-ounce cans of Mickey's Fine Malt Liquor, a regional and decidedly downmarket product from the Miller Brewing Company, but it was hardly a big moneymaker or a way to raise one's profile.

Spencer managed to get GSP signed to the Creative Artists Agency, which handles such bankable sports figures as David Beckham, Derek Jeter, LeBron James, Tony Hawk and Sidney Crosby. "I intentionally steered away from fight-specific brands to keep him clean," Spencer said. "That's also why I reached out to CAA and cultivated that relationship, because I knew that the sport was still struggling to gain mainstream acceptance, and having the backing of a powerhouse like CAA could certainly accelerate the process of getting Georges in front of the bigger brands."

At the time, neither GSP nor Spencer was truly aware of how popular the fighter was in a global context. But it really hit home when they traveled with Chuck Liddell to the Philippines on a promotional tour. Because mixed martial arts has a long history and is so popular there—truly part of the mainstream conscious-ness—UFC events are broadcast over the airwaves. In Manila, GSP's face is as familiar as Wayne Gretzky's is in Edmonton or Derek Jeter's is in New York. When he arrived there, he couldn't walk even a few feet without attracting a crowd of admirers. "It was like Beatlemania," Spencer said. "Georges is well received in the States and in Canada, but it was a whole different level in the Philippines . . . I was told how big the UFC was in the Philippines and how gracious they were—and they are the most gracious peo-ple on the planet—but the reception was beyond what Georges or myself ever expected." Returning home, she looked him up on Google and Yahoo! and found that he was by far the most popular mixed martial arts fighter in the world.

She knew GSP was an easily marketable product, handsome, intelligent, personable and modest with no skeletons in his closet. He wasn't the problem. Mainstream acceptance of mixed martial arts was. Or at least what major corporate advertisers thought mainstream acceptance of mixed martial arts was. Her mission was to change that perception.

There was another problem. In eight fights spanning January 2004 to December 2007, the UFC's welterweight title went from Matt Hughes to BJ Penn, back to Hughes, then to GSP to Serra to GSP again, and there were two interim titles in that span. Big-time advertisers wanted sports figures who were champions with staying power, not a guy who can win a title only to lose it a month or two later.

Defending his belt, especially against a worthy opponent, would do a lot to cement GSP's image as a champ among corporate bigwigs. Luckily, the planners at the UFC organized just such a match. Jon Fitch was another in a long line of outstanding college wrestlers from the Midwest (in this case, Fort Wayne, Indiana) to move to professional mixed martial arts fighting.

Fitch had a hard time at the start of his MMA career. Starting out as a light heavyweight (up to 205 pounds), he was fighting men with much bigger frames than his. He went 2–2, but showed great potential. Realizing his natural fighting weight was much lower, he switched to the middleweight class (up to 185 pounds). His first middleweight fight—at HOOK 'n' SHOOT: Boot Camp 1.1 in Evansville, Indiana, on March 8, 2003, for a small, regional organization that now specializes in women fighters—began well, but ended as a no contest when his opponent, Solomon "The King" Hutcherson was disqualified for kicking him in the face.

But it was the beginning of a major turnaround. He fought twice more as a middleweight, winning both fights. Then, in November

2003, he made his debut as a welterweight, forcing Shonie "Mr. International" Carter to submit. That was part of an incredible 17-fight undefeated streak in which he won victories over such notables as Carter, Josh "The People's Warrior" Burkman, Thiago "Pitbull" Alves and Diego "The Nightmare" Sanchez. By the time he was scheduled to meet GSP at *UFC 87: Seek and Destroy* in Minneapolis on August 9, 2008, he was 18–2 (with one no contest) and a more than worthy contender.

Before the fight, he appeared on the popular science show *MythBusters* to test if it was actually possible for a person to punch his or her way out of a coffin as Uma Thurman's character had in the movie *Kill Bill: Vol. 2*, even though his background and strength was in wrestling, not boxing. Limited by the space inside the coffin, Fitch managed to prove that it could happen and registered over 1,400 pounds of punching force. Just for fun, the *MythBusters* guys later measured the force behind Fitch's best punch, the right roundhouse. It came in at over 7,000 pounds of force. Still, GSP was a prohibitive favorite—at GSP -265/Fitch +205—with oddsmakers.

Many people considered BJ Penn, as a former welterweight champion, to be a more natural opponent for GSP, but he had shifted down to the lightweight (up to 155 pounds) class and was its current champ. He had won the title at *UFC 80: Rapid Fire* against Joe "Daddy" Stevenson and defended it at *UFC 84: Ill Will* against Sean Sherk. More than a few fans attributed Penn's return to the lightweight class to his reluctance to fight GSP again.

Dana White and analyst Joe Rogan did their best to hype the GSP–Fitch fight. Both fighters said the right things. GSP pointed out that Fitch definitely belonged in the ring with him—repeatedly calling him "the most dangerous" fighter he'd ever seen—but was sure he'd still leave the ring with his hand in the air.

To his credit, Fitch didn't play a role before the fight. He spoke about how a number of prominent welterweights had quietly declined to fight him, and said that he took that as a compliment. And he was smart enough to work out closely with Josh Koscheck, who didn't beat GSP, but fought him tough for three full rounds.

UFC 87 was an easy sell. Not only had Minneapolis never hosted a UFC event before, but the main event was a title fight featuring the already very popular GSP. Adding even more excitement was the fact that Brock "The Next Big Thing" Lesnar—a bona fide former WWE star who came from nearby South Dakota—was also in the mix. He was supposed to have fought UFC hall-of-famer Mark "The Hammer" Coleman, but when Coleman suffered an Achilles tendon injury, he was replaced by Heath "Texas Crazy Horse" Herring. A former Pride heavyweight champion, Herring was nonetheless extremely popular (especially in Japan) for his dramatic entrances and engaging personality. He is now pursuing an acting career as well as fighting.

The Target Center in Minneapolis was filled to capacity with over 15,000 fans with a $2.52 million gate and a 625,000 pay-per-view buy rate.

Before the GSP–Fitch fight, hall-of-famer lightweight Rob "The Saint" Emerson had the crowd on its feet with a nasty knockout of youngster Manvel "Pitbull" Gamburyan on his first punch. Then Lesnar completely dominated Herring in a three-round 30–26 unanimous decision.

When he arrived, Fitch looked the part. Wearing a wild T-shirt from Hostility and a baseball cap, he strode confidently, smiling the whole way. As with fellow Midwesterner Matt Hughes, Fitch preferred country music for his entrance, but went a little more upscale, selecting Johnny Cash's classic "Rusty Cage."

GSP had another new entrance song. "Boulbi" by French rapper Booba is a controversial song about growing up on the mean streets of Boulogne-Billancourt, a densely populated suburb of Paris. It wouldn't make the Top 40 charts in Minneapolis, but its throbbing bass kept most of the fans excited. As usual, he came out in a gi and rising-sun headband—one prefight commentator said, "It's hard not to like GSP when you see him come out in his little *Karate Kid* outfit"—but this time, his gi was black instead of blue and instead of being festooned with tons of patches from low-ball sponsors, all it had was a giant fleur-de-lis on the back. Given both a Canadian and a Québécois flag on his stride down, he threw them both up in the air.

Fitch came out punching. GSP went for his legs, putting him on the ground less than four seconds in. Fitch set up full guard, tied up both GSP's arms and managed to sneak a quick elbow to his face. The crowd was chanting "GSP! GSP!" Fitch, whose guard had never been passed in his UFC career, continued to look confident on his back, clearly looking for a way to effect an arm bar.

Moments later, the two were boxing when Fitch sent in a low kick. GSP took the opportunity to throw a huge right hand, sending a surprised Fitch back to the canvas. The challenger quickly recovered, getting to his knees before GSP pounced and laid in a startling combination of lefts and rights. Although breaking GSP's lock, Fitch still absorbed blow after blow thrown by GSP. Unable to stand, he rolled onto his back. GSP, from one knee, continued his barrage of punches. Commentators Goldberg and Rogan were talking like it was over. GSP just kept pounding him, and was now doing it with his elbows, a weapon that had proven far more effective than his fists over the years.

Fitch found a bit of second wind and began to fight back. But after a hard combination to his face, Fitch went down again, falling forward in what may have been a halfhearted takedown attempt.

On his hands and knees, Fitch took more shots to the head. Back on his back and in full guard, Fitch took repeated elbows to his face. His face was bleeding and he rolled to maintain half-guard. Then GSP did what no other UFC fighter had ever done—he passed Fitch's guard. But, unable to isolate an arm, GSP decided to keep punching. Fitch lasted until the horn. After one of the most lopsided rounds in UFC history, Fitch's men worked hard to stop the bleeding above his eye.

Round Two started out with boxing. GSP tried to grab Fitch's leg, but received a knee to the gut in rebuttal. He sent in a good jab, but Fitch answered with a solid right hook. GSP faked a Superman punch and delivered a right leg kick. Both fighters got some punches in, and GSP landed an inside calf kick. Then he landed a double jab, but missed the opportunity to deliver a combination. The two then traded jabs and GSP landed a couple of small kicks. Fitch landed a combination, then followed up with a flurry of short punches. GSP backed up and launched a powerful left hand. A couple of high kicks just grazed Fitch, then the horn sounded. GSP looked to have won the round, but not decisively.

Fitch landed the first punch of the third round—a hard right—but it cost him. GSP countered with a right hook that sent Fitch tumbling to the canvas. The punch sent his mouthpiece flying into the crowd. GSP pounced and took him down. Eventually, Fitch got on his hands and knees with GSP on top, riding him. It looked very much like GSP was going to try a rear-naked choke, but Fitch rolled him over. From his own back, GSP was still looking for a choke. But Fitch got up and mounted GSP, who established full guard. Goldberg pointed out that in over 132 minutes of UFC fighting, GSP had been on his back for less than five. Taking advantage of this opportunity, Fitch started battering him with big rights to the body. GSP looked powerless, and referee Yves Lavigne twice had to warn him not to grab the fence to help himself back up. As vulnerable as GSP was at this point, as Fitch got to his knees for extra punching power, GSP wriggled out, grabbed Fitch's left calf, lifted it and had him on his back in one swift move. With Fitch's head mashed against the fence, GSP started his own ground-and-pound assault. Fitch was bleeding again. He got to his knees and took a hard knee to the face.

Round Four started a little more auspiciously for Fitch. He landed a right that opened a cut just above GSP's left eye. As he was wiping blood from his face, Fitch sent in a nasty body kick and shot in for a takedown, but GSP's sprawl was too solid. GSP then sent in a body kick that may have landed just below the belt. Lavigne rushed in, but the two fighters tapped gloves and resumed. Fitch started landing his jabs, but GSP returned them, making full use of his slight reach advantage. Fitch fell onto his knees, gripping GSP's leg. Then GSP was on top of him. GSP isolated one of Fitch's legs and established a lock, but the horn sounded before Fitch came close to tapping.

That set up a final round in which Fitch—clearly behind in points—would have to knock the champ out or force him to submit. At the break, Lavigne called a doctor over to look at Fitch, who declared him fit to continue.

In the final round, GSP dominated. Fitch would occasionally try to get up, only to be dragged down again. The horn finally, mercifully sounded with GSP standing, carrying a helpless Fitch by one arm and one leg.

GSP was too tired to do his traditional celebratory backflip. Instead, he circled around the Octagon until he caught Fitch's eye. He approached him and fell to his knees, bowing his head. Fitch grabbed his hands and followed suit. They hugged, shook hands and exchanged a few words. Both men were cleaned up by cornermen. GSP was bloodied; Fitch looked like he had been hit by a truck.

As announcer Bruce Buffer declared the unanimous decision—one judge scored it 50–43, the other two 50–44—GSP
and Fitch spoke with each other. Then Fitch, looking very tired,
picked GSP up and clumsily carried him around the Octagon.
The crowd went nuts. Rogan entered the ring. GSP congratulated
Fitch, said he was "awesome," and said the loss was "probably the
best thing that could happen to him . . . [it will] make him stronger." He apologized for drinking and spitting out water and told
Rogan, "I'm ready to fight whoever deserves a shot . . . I know BJ
Penn wants it—I'll do it, he deserves it." Penn then entered the
ring, shook GSP's hand, congratulated him and said, "Let's do
this."

CHAPTER

But business was business, and GSP had to do a little more convincing to get the mainstream sponsors hooked. Fitch certainly was a tough opponent, but a title defense against a bigger-name fighter would do a lot more to solidify his status as a marketable brand. And, as everyone in the mixed martial arts world knew, the logical opponent was former champ BJ "The Prodigy" Penn.

Of course, GSP had beaten Penn in their earlier meeting at *UFC 58*, but it was a split decision with one judge actually giving the fight to Penn. GSP won the fight, but Penn had sent him to the hospital.

Since then, Penn had won the lightweight belt, beating Joe "Daddy" Stevenson and then former champs Jens Pulver and Sean Sherk (whose title was stripped after testing positive for anabolic steroids) to defend it. With Hughes and Serra out of the running, and fighters like Koscheck and Fitch not up to the task, it looked like the only fighter in the world with a realistic hope of unseating GSP was Penn.

In a cheeky and somewhat risky move, Dana White scheduled *UFC 94: St-Pierre vs. Penn 2* for January 31, 2009—the night before Super Bowl XLIII—at the MGM Grand Arena in Las Vegas. The number of pay-per-view subscriptions sold would be a good barometer of how popular mixed martial arts had become as a mainstream sport. If the UFC could get a decent number of people to shell out for a pay-per-view show the night before about 150 million people were going to spend their Sunday watching the big game, MMA would have to be taken more seriously. And it would prove that GSP, the champ, the guy whose name was on the marquee, was a legitimate sell.

Even though Penn was hardly known for his diplomacy, both men avoided trash-talking before the fight, instead respectfully praising their opponent's abilities and pointing out that the two best fighters were going to be in the ring and that the better fighter would have his hand in the air when it was over. As he had many times before, GSP pointed out how the loss to Serra changed his career, his friends, his outlook on life. He spoke about it the way an evangelist does about his faith. He also pointed out that much of the purported rivalry between the two was hype. He said he didn't hate Penn, that it was business. For his part, Penn pointed out that he hadn't studied GSP's fight against Fitch in detail because he was too busy rooting for GSP. GSP claimed that he didn't fight for fame or money, but for a lasting legacy. "I'm not going to lie," smiled Penn. "I fight for fame and money . . . and the people of Hawaii."

The hype hardly stopped with the fighters. Dana White claimed that the second GSP–Penn fight would be talked about "50 years from now." Online mixed martial arts magazine *Sherdog* agreed, naming it the most anticipated fight of the year. The mainstream sports media that had so shunned the UFC and mixed martial arts in the past were also getting into the excitement, with the likes of NBC Sports and *Sports Illustrated* discussing the upcoming fight.

And, for the first time, White publicly spoke about GSP (if he won the fight) facing Anderson "The Spider" Silva—the UFC's middleweight champion, who he called a better fighter than either welterweight. He said it could be a possibility in the future, but whoever won on January 31 would have to face Brazilian welter-weight Thiago Alves, who established himself as a contender after consecutive victories over Chris Lytle, Karo Parisyan, Hughes and Koscheck.

Penn—who, like GSP, has an easily chantable name—entered as always to "'E Ala 'E,'" a Hawaiian nationalist song by Israel "IZ" Ka'ano'i Kamakawiwo'ole, and a blast of crowd noise. The crowd greeted GSP even more loudly, as he entered to French rapper Sinik's "L'Homme a Abattre," another song about growing up tough in and around Paris and about how success comes only from inner strength. The referee was Herb Dean, a well-respected heavyweight fighter who had been refereeing since *UFC 48*.

Again, Penn looked softer than GSP, especially around the middle, as a result of moving up a weight class after fighting 13 pounds lighter for the past year and a half.

Penn immediately came out attacking low. The resulting clinch allowed the fighters to trade repeated knees to the midsections and thighs. After almost a minute, GSP grabbed Penn's right thigh to effect a single-leg takedown. But Penn was elusive—with Dean repeatedly warning GSP not to grab Penn's shorts—and steadied himself on the fence to beat it. GSP gave up on the takedown, pushed Penn up against the fence and started punching. Penn re-plied with attempts at taking GSP's front leg out from under him to no avail. GSP then tried Penn's right thigh again, pulling him away from the supporting fence, which allowed Penn a few shots at his unprotected head. Back against the fence, Penn broke the clinch and delivered a hard shot to GSP's head.

GSP, taking the center of the Octagon, looked more aggressive, sending in jabs and kicks that didn't do much damage, but left Penn on the defensive.

Both men traded jabs before GSP landed a nasty right-left combination to Penn's face. A few more jabs and GSP clinched up again, pushing Penn back to the fence. Penn struggled out of it and the men started boxing again. GSP landed a kick to Penn's high inner thigh and followed it up with a big outside kick to the same thigh. The round ended with both men standing, looking for an opening.

Round Two saw Penn strike first with a pair of left hooks. GSP went into a protective clinch, and the crowd loudly communicated its disapproval. GSP then hooked his leg around Penn's and sent him down to the mat. Penn established a rubber guard, which prevented GSP from mounting any offense, but GSP passed it into half-guard and side control. Working to isolate Penn's left arm, GSP also got a few punches in. Penn reestablished full guard to eliminate the arm bar or kimura threat, but that left him wide open to the ground-and-pound. GSP passed, but Penn reestablished guard. Penn had spent the whole time since GSP passed his initial rubber guard on the ground, receiving an ugly beating, especially from GSP's left fist and elbow. He was bleeding from below his left eye when the horn sounded.

Taking advantage of Penn's cut face, GSP opened the third round with a series of hard jabs to his nose and cheeks. That started Penn's nose bleeding. Defending against the punches left Penn's body open and GSP shot in for a takedown. Penn could only establish half guard. While GSP was concentrating on blows to the face,

Penn moved into full guard. From above, GSP started delivering hammerfists—a strike from the bottom meaty part of the fist that protects the puncher's hand bones and concentrates the force the opponent receives to the point where facial bones can be broken.

Penn struggled and finally managed to get out from under GSP. Once up, he grabbed GSP's thigh for a takedown attempt, but GSP shook him off and pulled him down to the ground again. Though Penn was guarded, GSP delivered withering blows from his left fist and elbow until the horn sounded.

Round Four started with Penn blocking a low kick, leaving himself open to the following jab. He then threw a jab of his own, but GSP easily got under it and sent Penn back down with a two-arm takedown. GSP then passed Penn's guard with remarkable quickness. From side control, GSP started hammering Penn's mid-section with his knee. While attempting to get on top of Penn, GSP smashed a hard elbow to his face to quell any offense from him. Penn established guard, but GSP passed it again.

Back in side control, GSP continued to pummel Penn's head. With Penn unable to defend, referee Dean came in close, deciding whether or not to give GSP the TKO. But when he saw Penn adequately and intelligently defending himself, he backed off and the horn sounded with GSP's fists and elbows still pounding away.

As soon as Penn, bloody and wobbly, got to his corner, he hung from the fence. His cornermen asked him if he knew where he was, then summoned the doctors to check him out. He was too injured to continue. Referee Dean announced that GSP had won by TKO on doctor's advice at the end of the fourth round. GSP saluted the crowd and then went to see if Penn was okay. GSP spoke to him as his men wiped the blood from his face and a doctor shone a light into his eyes to check for a concussion. GSP then walked to the center of the ring, saluted the crowd and was mobbed by his cornermen. The crowd of them, arms on each other's shoulders, started dancing and singing "Olé, Olé, Olé!"

After the fight, Rogan declared it "the biggest fight in mixed martial arts history" and congratulated him. "Last time I fought him, I won in a decision, and this time I wanted to take him out," said GSP. "And I did it. He's very tough." Then they brought Alves out. He congratulated GSP on a great fight and told him he was a big fan.

GSP had beaten Penn again. He had defended his title for a second time against the last real threat to it. He took home a minimum of $400,000 and had moved on to another level.

*   *   *

Two big things happened to GSP after the Penn fight: one bad and the other quite good. The bad one happened first.

Two days after the bout, Penn's older brother JD announced that he would be making a formal complaint to the Nevada State Athletic Commission (NSAC) accusing GSP of covering his body with an illegal substance—a petroleum jelly named Vaseline. Vaseline has many uses and is legal in mixed martial arts (as well as other sports), where its ability to help stop cuts from bleeding is useful, but it's primarily a lubricant. A fighter with Vaseline on his body would have a tremendous advantage—being slippery, his opponent would not be able to apply holds or locks or have traction on takedown attempts.

The elder Penn cited the official video of the event. Between the first and second rounds, GSP's cornerman and muay Thai coach, Phil Nurse, can be seen applying Vaseline to GSP's eyelids and eyebrows, which is perfectly legal, but then, without wiping off his hands, he touches the fighter's back. The Penn camp pointed out that with Vaseline on his back, GSP would be almost impossible to hold on to.

"We are not trying to make excuses, but the NSAC needs to protect the fighters," the elder Penn said. "They never notified us or completely wiped his back with water and towels."

It was a serious accusation that could have led to GSP's disqualification, his title being stripped and even suspension or expulsion from the organization. Fans were divided. Some said GSP was a cheat and that the UFC tolerated it because he was so popular, while others accused Penn of being a sore loser, looking to rationalize his poor performance in the fight.

Surprisingly, White weighed in *against* his star fighter, but didn't blame him directly. "Do I think that he got greased? Yeah, I do, absolutely, 100 percent, I think that that guy was rubbing grease on him," he said. "Do I think Georges was trying to cheat? Absolutely not at all, but that cornerman was rubbing grease on him. You cannot do that." And he added that while the Vaseline on him would be illegal, it didn't affect the outcome of the match. "He didn't have to put grease on him. Georges St-Pierre was winning the fight," he said. "He was dominant in the stand up and on the ground. To have a fight or a fighter like St-Pierre tainted over a stupidity, I hate it. It sucks."

But the accusations mounted. Penn's head coach, Rudy Valentino, stated that GSP appeared "greased up" in their first fight at *UFC 58* and again in his victory against Matt Serra at *UFC 83*. Even Jason Miller, who lost to GSP at *UFC 52*, got into the discussion. He claimed that when he fought GSP, he noticed that he was greasy and mentioned it to referee John McCarthy. He claimed that McCarthy told him to "shut up." He also said that he pursued the issue through official channels with no success and predicted that Penn would have the same fate. "We [went] all the way up to the commission and from me getting beat up in the second round saying, 'Hey, this guy is greased up,' to BJ taking it all the way to the Nevada State Athletic Commission and them still saying, 'Nah,'" he said. "Look, don't have the rule if you're not going to enforce it. Don't even have the rule. Let's just cover ourselves in baby oil and let's fight. Let's do it. Like, I didn't really care. I would fight Georges with a tire iron. We both have a tire iron and a trash can lid and I'd fight him like that. But that's not the rules. The rules are: don't grease yourself up, and he broke them, but no one gives a damn."

Penn registered a 20-page complaint that requested GSP's license be suspended or revoked, the fight be declared a no contest and among other things, large amounts of cash be paid by various people in GSP's camp, including Nurse and head coach Greg Jackson.

Jackson, speaking for the team, denied any wrongdoing and said that Nurse's actions were part of a technique used to aid GSP's breathing and that any residual Vaseline transferred to his back was minute and inadvertent. He also claimed that when it was brought to his attention that there may be a foreign substance on GSP's back, he wiped the fighter off.

GSP didn't say much about the controversy at the time, aside from his official statement: "If there was any Vaseline left on his hand after he put it on my face, it was unintentional, and I do not believe it made the slightest difference in the outcome of the fight." Later, he did speak to *Sports Illustrated*. "I haven't seen the fight yet, but I remember at some point something happened and the athletic commission was complaining," he told them. "They used a towel to wet my back and wipe it off. I don't mind. I didn't put Vaseline on myself and I'm not a cheater." He extended an olive branch to Penn, offering a rematch.

On March 19, 2009, the NSAC held a formal hearing. Penn was there, represented by his mother, Lorraine Shin, and his lawyer, Raffi Nahabedian. GSP did not attend, instead sending his legal team and his coaches. Nurse and Jackson both apologized to Penn, but denied they intentionally did anything wrong. At the hearing's conclusion, NSAC executive director Keith Kizer decided to take no disciplinary action against GSP or his team, but he did not officially close the case. Penn, who said he undertook the campaign to "clean up the sport" and prevent injuries, was bitter. "The ultimate vindication would be a rematch and to kick his butt," he said. "A good vindication would be a fair rematch; and if he beats me fairly, I'll be the first to shake his hand."

* * *

With what the media called "Greasegate" behind him, GSP was free to move forward. And that's when something good happened.

His reputation intact, GSP was a much bigger star than the UFC had ever seen before. He was in big-time demand. He even was hired to teach a few moves to Sheikh Tahnoon bin Zayed Al Nahyan, son of former United Arab Emirates president Sheikh Zayed bin Sultan Al Nahyan, who was a big fan.

It wasn't just fight fans who noticed. The corporate world finally officially recognized GSP. At the end of March 2009, Gatorade announced that GSP would appear in its television, online and print ads in Canada. Terms of the deal were not disclosed, but were thought to be huge by Canadian standards, as CAA rarely brokered deals that didn't reach into seven digits. "Georges St-Pierre truly embodies the spirit of athleticism for Canada, from his grueling behind-the-scenes training regimen to his championship fights in front of the world," said Dale Hooper, vice president for marketing at PepsiCo Beverages Canada, distributor of Gatorade.

"We're very proud to be associated with an athlete like GSP who is such a motivation to any Canadian who sweats."

As big a deal as it was, Spencer did not stop with Gatorade. On November 4, 2009, Under Armour enthusiastically announced that GSP would be the face of its very popular BoxerJock and BoxerBrief underwear brands, as well as one of the primary faces for its Recharge post-workout suit. "Not only is Georges one of the biggest stars in one of the fastest growing sports in the world, but his dedication to training and making himself the best at what he does aligns perfectly with our brand's mission to make all athletes better," said Steve Battista, Under Armour's senior vice president for branding. "When we found out that he was a fan of ours, we jumped on the opportunity to bring him into the Under Armour family." He later referred to GSP as the "Michael Jordan" of mixed martial arts.

As always, GSP was more modest than his supporters. "It is quite an honor for me to represent Under Armour," was his official statement. "I have always appreciated the quality of their products, and to be partners with them is a dream come true."

His out-of-the-Octagon career took yet another turn. GSP became friends with a man named Hector Echavarria, who turned to muay Thai on the advice of a police officer who caught him street fighting in his native Argentina. He had a long and storied career as a fighter with the United States Kickboxing Association, eventually making the United States Martial Arts Hall of Fame. As his fighting career wound down, he started teaching. He started with the public, then specialized in celebrities like model Kendra Wilkinson and boxer Hector "Macho" Camacho before adding mixed martial arts clients like Quinton "Rampage" Jackson and Cheick Kongo.

In 1987, Echavarria met a woman named Carol Meyers, who worked for *Miami Vice*, one of the most popular shows of the time.

She was so taken with him that she asked him to be on the show as a guest for an episode. He caught the eye of Argentine producer Carlos Mentasti, who cast him in a trio of action comedies—*Los extermineitors*, *Extermineitors II: La venganza del dragon* and *Extermineitors III: La gran pelea final*—that were huge box office hits throughout South America. That was followed by a long run as one of the lead actors in *Brigada cola*, an immensely popular action comedy about a Buenos Aires SWAT team that has been described as a "Latin American *A-Team*."

Back in the United States, Echavarria did some more acting in low-budget films he also produced. The films—beginning with action movies *Extreme Force*, *The Falkland Man*, *Confessions of a Pit Fighter* and horror movie *Lake Dead*—contained lots of violence and gratuitous nudity, were not well received by critics and were generally released straight to video.

In 2009, he managed to get backing from Vancouver-area concert promoter Destiny Entertainment Inc. for *Never Surrender*, a film he was to write, produce and star in. He described the plot on his website: "From the cage to the big screen, the world's greatest Mixed Martial Arts Champions come together for the first time in a major motion picture. When an MMA world champion is lured into the illegal world of underground cage fighting by an elusive promoter, he quickly realizes that the only way out is to kill or to be killed. In a place where some fight for glory and some fight for the fight; he will fight for his life. Now, in his greatest effort to come out on top, he can never look back; never show weakness, never leave . . . and NEVER SURRENDER." (The capitalization is his.)

The cast featured a number of UFC fighters, including Anderson Silva, BJ Penn, Quinton Jackson, Heath Herring and even GSP. Filmed mostly in a north Toronto warehouse, GSP played a small role as Georges, one of the fighters Echavarria's character had to defeat on his way out.

Never Surrender went straight to video but was a moderate success for distributor Lionsgate. It was followed up by *Hell's Chain,* in which GSP played Stone, a slightly bigger role than he had in *Never Surrender,* with similar results.

Echavarria made a third movie in 2009, *Death Warrior.* It also featured GSP and a number of other mixed martial artists. GSP's role, as Shaman, was much bigger this time, and he seemed pretty comfortable in it. When asked by a Canadian reporter on the set if he wanted to do more acting, GSP replied: "Absolutely, but with my fighting career I have to limit myself to small roles. I think it's going to be a good after-career for me." Spencer agreed, saying she didn't mind his getting involved in film but that it wouldn't affect his day job. "It hasn't been a priority at this point," she said of his acting.

His actual career and top priority came calling again in 2009, though. As promised, White set GSP up with a fight against Alves at *UFC 100,* to be held at Mandalay Bay on July 11.

* * *

While things were going well for GSP, they were not for his old friend, sparring partner and erstwhile cornerman David Loiseau. Although he had an 18–9 professional record heading into 2009, he had gone just 3–4 in the UFC and had been released from the organization.

He still wanted to keep fighting, though, and perhaps return to the UFC. He became involved in a new Montreal-based mixed martial arts organization called the XMMA (another company, Australia's Xtreme MMA, is also sometimes called the XMMA, but is not related). He became president and had a significant interest in the company. But he found the job very demanding and decided to return to training and fighting full-time. So he sold the company and put it behind him, eventually re-signing with the UFC to fight in *UFC 113: Machida vs. Shogun 2*, slated for May 8, 2010 in Montreal.

Loiseau didn't sell XMMA to just anybody. He sold it to Burton Rice, who operates a company called Brand-U Media out of the Kahnawake Mohawk Reserve. His flagship product is a thick, glossy magazine called *Naked Eye* that is aimed at the 18–35 demographic. It was first launched in 1999, but lasted just one issue due to a shortage of ad revenue. It was relaunched in 2007 and has been published quarterly since, but many contributors have complained of harsh treatment and not being paid, according to *Masthead*, a trade magazine covering the Canadian publishing industry. Brand-U Media also owns Headrush, a clothing company with the slogan "death B4 defeat."

But that, and the now defunct XMMA, don't appear to have been Rice's only businesses. On June 3, 2009, more than 600 officers from the Montreal police, the Sûreté du Quebec, the RCMP and Kahnawake Peacekeepers participating in Project SharQc, which targeted organized crime in the province, launched a series of raids against Hells Angels and their associates. One of their many raids was on a heavily fortified warehouse with magnetic doors, security guards and a 10-foot-high fence on Old Chateauguay Road in Kahnawake.

Inside, they found $3.4 million in cash and three guns among copies of *Naked Eye*. In the entire operation, the police seized 34,800 pounds of tobacco, 1 kilo of cocaine, 860 rocks of crack, 900 grams of marijuana, 4,000 tablets of methamphetamine, an undetermined quantity of ecstasy, 12 firearms, 11 safes, 19 computers, several bulletproof vests and promotional material of the Hells Angels.

Rice, his younger brother Francis, his father Peter and *Naked Eye*'s director of operations Michel LeBlanc were among the arrested. Rice was charged with gangsterism, fraud exceeding $5,000 and conspiracy.

Police alleged that they were part of a scheme that sold illegal cigarettes—a huge business for organized crime in Canada, where taxes can make legal cigarettes cost twice or even triple what they do in the United States—and that the Hells Angels had used the warehouse not just to store their cigarettes and drugs but also to hold top-level meetings.

While Loiseau was not charged with any crime or even mentioned in the evidence, the Quebec Athletic Commission denied him a licence because of his "associations with organized crime." Loiseau said that after he sold the XMMA, he had no decision-making presence with its new owners and had no idea what else they were involved with. He didn't take the decision well, writing on his Facebook page: "10 years of my life to the sport of MMA. Opened doors for Quebec fighters, put Quebec on the map, helped build the sport in Quebec. Now the Quebec commission wont let me fight . . . UNACCEPTABLE." He was replaced at *UFC 113* by fellow-Canadian Jason MacDonald, who was knocked out by Alabama-native John Salter.

An interesting side note is that without GSP as a headliner, *UFC 113* put just 17,647 people in Bell Centre seats for a $3.27 million gate, far less than the 23,190 people who paid $5.1 million to see him fight Serra there at *UFC 83*.

Loiseau would later fight at *UFC 115: Liddell vs. Franklin* in Vancouver, where he was knocked out by Brazilian Mario "Super Mario" Miranda. It probably put his career in the UFC on hold.

*   *   *

The hype surrounding the GSP-Alves bout was huge. It was the co-main event at *UFC 100* and the heavyweight title bout featured the return of champion Brock Lesnar, now recovered from abdominal surgery, against interim champion Frank Mir. Ticket prices averaged out to $524 and led to an announced gate of $5,128,490, the second largest in UFC history. The pay-per-view buy rate of 1.6 million set a new UFC record.

Few would disagree that Alves had won the right to be there. He had an 18–4 record, but was actually better than it would indicate. At the outset of his professional career, Alves was a pure striker with poor takedown and wrestling skills. But once he developed those skills, he became a welterweight force, taking a seven-fight win streak into the Octagon. He had recently beaten Matt Hughes by knockout at *UFC 85* and had prevented Hughes from taking him down even once. And he was still just 25 years old.

Neither man engaged in trash talk, staying polite, positive and eminently likeable. If anything, Alves seemed in awe of the champ, almost the same way that GSP was when he first fought Hughes five years earlier.

For his part, GSP commented that Alves was his toughest opponent so far, echoing sentiments he had expressed earlier about Fitch and others. When ESPN asked GSP if he was going to do his "breathing exercises" (a veiled reference to Greasegate), he paused and responded by saying that he would, but that he would be thoroughly checked for foreign substances. "I've never cheated in my life; I'm not a cheater," he said calmly. "I'm a proud champion and I want to win fair and square. I don't mind if they double-check me . . . it's even better for me, I'm happy." Other reporters cited the many distractions in his life, with commercials, photo shoots and even acting in movies taking a significant chunk of his time and energy. GSP replied only by saying he was a more mature person now and that he wouldn't let anything get in the way of staying champion.

Because the first eight bouts took longer than anticipated, the undercard fight between Jon Fitch and Paulo Thiago was postponed until after the two title fights. When it was his time, Alves entered to his theme song, "Big Things Poppin'," a cleaned-up version of Atlanta rapper T.I.'s hit "Big Shit Poppin'." He looked huge for a 170-pounder. Like all professional mixed martial artists, Alves loses weight to fight, but unlike GSP who walks around at about 185 pounds, Alves's street weight is closer to, and sometimes in excess of, 200.

As usual, GSP came out to French-language hip-hop. But instead of another Parisian, his song at *UFC 100* was from a Montrealer. Born in Haiti under the name S. Rimsky Salgado, Imposs is a popular and award-winning rapper most famous for nicknaming Montreal "Real City" and for collaborating with Wyclef Jean on his huge hit "24 Heures a Vivre." GSP picked one of his songs, "Mornier 4 Life," as his entrance music.

When he took off his gi, GSP was wearing red shorts with his new logo picked by his fans on his website—his initials shaped to look like a fleur-de-lis—on them. Alves wore fighter shorts with a design that featured the Brazilian flag.

The first and second rounds started with both fighters trading low kicks. In the second, GSP threw a Superman punch and took Alves down. Alves had only half guard, but nearly got away before GSP got back on top. Alves established full guard, but it cost him, as GSP straightened up and started dropping in huge punches. One of them opened up a cut on Alves's face.

GSP then passed guard into side mount. Alves reestablished guard with GSP back on top. With GSP trying to pass guard, Alves made a break for it and got standing by sheer will. GSP pushed him into the fence, holding him there until the horn sounded. It was clear that Alves's nose was bleeding.

Alves started Round Three aggressively with a quick rush, but GSP was ready and fought him off with a storm of punches, then a strong sprawl. Back to boxing, both fighters felt the other out before trading kicks to the body. When Alves paused to wipe the blood from his nose, GSP caught him with a left that sent him down to the canvas. Immediately, the champ was on top of him, setting up a classic ground-and-pound position. Alves managed to protect his head well, but didn't appear to be able to mount any offense of his own.

The crowd was hyped for the start of Round Four. GSP began the round with a quick inside leg kick. Alves absorbed it and moved toward the champ, showing takedown. But GSP caught him with a succession of quick jabs before shooting in himself and effecting a quick two-leg takedown. Alves escaped again as GSP was setting up, and turned the tables, hammering him with punches from above. GSP pulled Alves closer to reduce the range and power of his punches, then kicked his way out of the hold.

Now on their feet, Alves sent in an uppercut, but it was too slow. GSP ducked and got an easy takedown. In half guard, the strong challenger managed to get onto his knees. With GSP on his back, again working for the rear-naked choke, Alves was in pure defensive mode when the horn sounded again.

The final round began with GSP sending in a hard low kick and getting out of the way of the same kind of overhanded right that Koscheck repeatedly sent at him. GSP sent in a Superman punch that missed and had to recover quickly in order to block a head kick from Alves, then duck under a huge left. GSP dove into Alves while he was finishing his follow-through and got another quick and easy-looking takedown.

But again Alves pressed himself back to vertical, and they began boxing again. Before long, GSP shot in again and threw Alves back down. And, one more time, Alves muscled his way back to his feet only to be taken down. The crowd started going wild, they could see the clock, they knew it was over. Alves valiantly did his best to escape, but by then the end was inevitable. Just before the horn sounded, Alves struggled to his feet one last time.

The fight over, Alves lifted GSP's hand, indicating he knew who had won.

GSP had clearly won the fight. His strategy was outstanding. If Alves had one big advantage, it was as a striker, with his thick arms and legs capable of delivering withering blows. But he rarely connected. And when a big punch or kick attempt left him off balance, GSP was quickly in there for a takedown. Making it a more remarkable achievement is the fact that he reaggravated an old groin injury in the third round of the fight. It was obvious afterward when he was limping around the ring. "I was in real bad pain," he said. "It happened in the third round when I was on my back and he pushed my leg. It could have been a bad night for me if this thing turned bad."

After the fight, GSP said what a lot of people were thinking. He praised Alves and likened him to himself when he faced Matt Hughes. And, as with the recent victory over Penn, members of the mixed martial arts media and posters on online forums began to openly criticize GSP for beating, but not finishing off his opponent. They accused him of playing it safe to protect his title.

In the co-main event, Lesnar went on to beat Mir with a TKO from punches early in the second round. Fitch then beat Thiago to put himself back into the welterweight contenders' race.

* * *

The UFC scheduled a fourth title defense for GSP on March 27, 2010, at Newark, New Jersey's Prudential Center at *UFC 111: St-Pierre vs. Hardy*. His opponent would be lanky Englishman Dan Hardy. GSP politely referred to him as his toughest challenge yet. Oddsmakers disagreed, making GSP the prohibitive favorite. At GSP -800/Hardy +500, a winning bet on GSP would barely buy a cup of beer. GSP dominated the fight and successfully defended his title.

CHAPTER 12

After a few unsuccessful attempts to score a free ticket to GSP's historic fight at *UFC 124: St-Pierre vs. Koscheck 2* at Montreal's Bell Centre on December 11, 2010, this author finally had to break down and buy one. Of course since the event sold out almost instantaneously, I had to pay through the nose.

GSP was at the top of his game. A little more than eight months earlier, he had easily dispatched Dan Hardy for his 20th win as a professional.

I'd seen some partisan crowds before, but nothing like this. GSP's name and face were plastered all over Montreal. I heard plenty about him on radio and TV in both French and English, not to mention a lot of loathing for his opponent. And pretty well every guest in the hotel where I stayed, and every person in the surrounding neighborhood, was wearing something adorned with GSP's name or new logo. Plenty of them were also wearing souvenir headbands with a rising sun between a black fleur-de-lis and the letters "GSP." And Koscheck had done his best to keep the level of hype up, making disdainful comments to the media about GSP, Canadians and people of French ancestry.

It was tense. Dana White admitted that he had a plan with the Montreal police to handle a potential riot if GSP lost. He told reporters that Koscheck "better have a fucking helicopter waiting out front if he wins that fight ... and mine will be right next to it."

Inside the Bell Centre, many of the fans—the majority in fact—looked like the fighters themselves. Most of the men worked out (some to excess), had shaved heads, had tattoos and were dressed in Affliction, Hostility or other similar clothing. If I hadn't known the fighters better, I wouldn't have been surprised if any of about half of the fans took his shirt off and stepped into the Octagon. And if there was even one single man or boy in the entire audience whose hair was long enough to touch his shirt collar, I missed him.

The first match saw Halifax-born Laval-raised John "The Bull" Makdessi come out to thunderous applause. A kickboxing specialist who trains at Montreal's Tristar Gym alongside GSP, he was a crowd favorite. His opponent was a lightweight wrestling specialist who gave up modeling for Abercrombie & Fitch to pursue a career in the UFC. But Pat "Awesomely Awesome" Audinwood's boyish good looks couldn't help him as Makdessi controlled him for a one-sided unanimous decision.

The next five fights all featured Canadians. The UFC frequently adds fighters to the card who are from the area or country to card in a smart marketing effort to increase fan support. TJ Grant, a welterweight Brazilian jiu-jitsu specialist from Sidney Crosby's hometown of Cole Harbour, Nova Scotia, faced Brazilian Ricardo "Big Dog" Almeida. The Brazilian mopped the floor with him.

Toronto's Scott Pierson then beat Pennsylvanian Matt Riddle to hoots from the crowd. Kenora, Ontario's Jesse "Water" Bongfeldt (a last-minute replacement for injured Jason MacDonald, a Nova

Scotian) fought to a draw with Brazilian Rafael "Sapo" Natal, which angered the crowd. (A small controversy would arise later when it was indicated that one of the judges had actually awarded the fight to Natal, but it went in the record books as a draw.)

The partisan crowd was jubilant when Toronto-based lightweight Mark Bocek forced Kentucky's Dustin "McLovin" Hazelett to submit in the first round with a triangle choke. And it was bitterly disappointed when New Jersey's Dan Miller outpointed veteran Joe Doerksen, who's from a dot on the map in southern Manitoba.

The main card began with a fight that drew intense interest from much of the crowd. Welterweight contender Thiago Alves, who fought GSP in *UFC 100,* faced off against Boston-based John "Doomsday" Howard. Alves looked like the superior fighter, but appeared cautious—as though he was saving his best stuff for another night. But it was enough to get the unanimous decision.

The following bout ended quickly, with Mac Danzig knocking out Joe "Daddy" Stevenson less than two minutes into the first round.

The next fight was expected to be a great one as New Jersey's Jim Miller (Dan's brother) took on Brazilian Charles "do Bronx" Oliveira. Miller had an 18–2 record with a five-fight win streak that included victories over Danzig and Bocek. Oliveira was 14–0 with all but one victory coming from a submission or a knockout.

They didn't disappoint, coming out aggressively from the start. The fighters were evenly matched until Miller caught Oliveira in a knee bar, earning the submission just a tick less than two minutes into the match. The crowd cheered appreciatively and positively exploded when Miller, who has a reputation as a good guy, shouted, "Merci Montreal!" into Joe Rogan's microphone with an impeccable Québécois accent. It was a smart move than won him a lot of local fans.

The next fight was announced as the co-main event: Indiana's 6-foot-7 Sean "Big Sexy" McCorkle was taking on 6-foot-11 Stefan "Skyscraper" Struve from the Netherlands. Even though McCorkle had gone 10–0 and Struve had a 20–4 record, the battle of the giants wasn't a great fight. Neither fighter managed to land much, and the crowd started yelling "boring!" and impatiently chanting "GSP! GSP!" before the first round was even halfway over. The fight mercifully ended at 3:55 of the first round. Struve was on top and punching. He didn't appear to be doing any real damage, but since McCorkle wasn't even trying to escape, let alone do anything offensive, referee Yves Lavigne made the call.

During the wait for the main event, music and video featuring some of the best moves in UFC history kept us in our seats. Every time GSP appeared on screen, the crowd exploded. Every time Koscheck was shown, the crowd booed with vigor. Videos of interviews with both fighters followed. Whenever GSP's face was on screen, the crowd was so loud that the dialogue was drowned out. The same thing happened with boos when it was Koscheck's turn. Few forgot his prefight comment, "I can't wait to hear the sound of 23,000 French Canadians in total silence." He was, at least, right on the number. The 23,152 fans who packed the Bell Centre that night set a new UFC attendance record.

When the video came to a close, the boos began to crescendo. Then Koscheck's entrance music—"Higher Ground," the Red Hot Chili Peppers' tribute to Stevie Wonder—flooded the arena. When he finally appeared, the music could barely be heard. Koscheck was grinning and appealing to the crowd to boo louder, pantomiming that he couldn't hear them.

The UFC let him absorb the crowd's abuse for a surprisingly long time. The crowd started a chant—"Fuck you, Koscheck!"— which would continue to alternate with "GSP! GSP!" the rest of the night.

The opening strains of GSP's entrance song weren't familiar to many in the audience, it was "Ça Fait Mal," another ode to the tough Paris suburbs, this time by rapper La Fouine, but it riled them up even more than they had been for Koscheck. By the time their hero made it to the Octagon, La Fouine could no longer be heard over the shouting.

GSP opened the fight with a few quick jabs before launching a single-leg takedown attempt that Koscheck avoided of by retreating to the fence for support. GSP responded with more jabs and low kicks. The crowd cheered every one.

Sensing an opening, Koscheck sent in a combination, but missed on both. For his efforts, he received a nasty right to the face followed by two quick jabs before having to block a quick high kick.

The challenger finally got a short left in, but missed on a follow-up. Two more jabs hit his face. Koscheck went in for a takedown, but started slowly, allowing GSP time to defend. He tried it again, this time pushing GSP into a clinch against the fence. Unable to do much upstairs, Koscheck delivered a foot stomp. He then went low and managed a single-leg takedown, but it was too late to work further. The horn sounded with Koscheck on top of the champ, but it was clear the judges would award the round to GSP.

Once he got to his corner, it was apparent that Koscheck had suffered some damage in the first round. The area above and below his right eye was puffy and discolored, and it looked like he couldn't open the eye itself.

When the second round began, it was clear that Koscheck had trouble seeing out of his right eye. GSP took advantage with a quick Superman punch. Then he sent in a few low kicks, concentrating on Koscheck's blind side. Koscheck blindly sent in a right cross that came nowhere near the champ. Realizing he had to get in close, Koscheck kept rushing GSP, but paid for it by absorbing a steady stream of leg kicks and jabs.

Koscheck kept pressing and managed to land a right. GSP responded with a nasty uppercut, then a Superman punch. Realizing that his best chance to win was still in his powerful right hand, Koscheck kept trying with it, but GSP was too quick. GSP stayed on his feet, sending in safe jabs and low kicks of his own. Koscheck did manage to get close, but GSP kept jabbing as time ran out.

Round Three opened with GSP sending in a series of jabs, again at Koscheck's right eye. Koscheck was doing his best to block them and send in punches of his own, but had no defense for GSP's low kicks. GSP shot in, but Koscheck sprawled back. They clinched, and GSP sent in some knees to the abdomen. GSP went low, but Koscheck escaped. Back to boxing, GSP delivered a number of quick jabs. Koscheck tried to kick, but missed. It was clear he couldn't see at all from his right eye and was blindly sending in whatever he could. GSP looked at the clock before sending in more jabs and low kicks.

In between rounds, doctors attended to Koscheck, working on his solidly closed and swollen right eye. They talked to him, but he waved them off, indicating there was no way he was going to throw in the towel.

As soon as the fourth round started, GSP was aggressively in Koscheck's face. After a few quick punches and kicks, GSP went low for a takedown. On the mat, Koscheck groped for GSP's leg in a vain attempt at a knee bar. GSP snapped it from his grip and pushed Koscheck into the fence. Using it for support, Koscheck got both men to their feet. With an inconclusive clinch going on too long without any action, referee Herb Dean forced them to separate.

Back at the center of the cage, Koscheck continued sending in his signature overhand rights. They all missed except for one that just kissed GSP's cheek. GSP drove in more jabs and one hard one sent Koscheck tumbling to the mat. As he got up, GSP kept sending in leg kicks and hard left fists that Koscheck couldn't see, let alone defend. The round ended with Koscheck trying to stay on his feet while the champ hammered him from a distance.

As soon as he was seated, the doctors rushed up to Koscheck and worked on his eye. The crowd booed them lustily. They fell quiet when Koscheck again indicated that he was going back in to fight.

As the final round began, Koscheck approached the champ, who landed a huge overhand left to his now grossly swollen right eye. Dazed, Koscheck kept sending in his big overhand rights. GSP just kept on jabbing. He faked a takedown a couple of times, but stayed with a steady diet of jabs and low kicks. GSP had the fight well in hand. The crowd continued to taunt the helpless Koscheck, who could do little but hold his left fist in front of his face and throw his right one at the champ.

GSP then slammed him against the fence. In a clinch, Koscheck desperately tried to grab hold of anything. GSP threw him to the floor. Koscheck sprang back up. GSP knocked him back down. With just 30 seconds left, the crowd noise returned to incredible levels. Koscheck popped up again and launched a desperate spinning kick as his final attempt to win. It missed by a mile. GSP sent in a few more short punches, then got into a clinch.

I couldn't hear the horn because of the crowd noise, but I knew the fight was over when GSP let Koscheck go, started to pat him on the back and hugged him. Much of the crowd was hurling abuse at the badly beaten Koscheck, but GSP wasn't. The champ may have solidly controlled the fight, dominating the upstart in every aspect of the sport, but he realized that Koscheck never gave up. No matter what kind of pounding GSP gave him, he survived.

After GSP was announced as the winner, he took the microphone and thanked his fans. The cheering was once again unbearably loud. He told the crowd not to hate Koscheck, the things he said before their match were just to hype it, he wasn't really a bad guy. There were still a few boos, but they were drowned out by the applause.

It was later determined that one of GSP's first-round lefts had broken Koscheck's orbital bone and that he was indeed blind in the right eye for the duration of the fight. The injury caused air bubbles to form under his skin, which would have burst if he were to ride in an airplane. The UFC hired a driver to take him to Boston for treatment. He required corrective surgery and wouldn't be able to fight for almost a year afterward.

*   *   *

This second GSP–Koscheck fight showed not just what was great about GSP, but also a few things that are wrong about the UFC. Despite the many abusive and personal things Koscheck said before the fight, GSP never stooped at all. Instead, he remained gentlemanly and generous, while still quite confident.

And when it came time to fight, he did. Dominating in every aspect and right from the opening, GSP was as gracious as could be imagined, praising his lesser opponent and imploring his fans to show compassion and understanding to a young man who had earned his respect if not theirs.

But even before the fight was over, mixed martial arts forums were alive with fans complaining that GSP was being cautious and "playing just to win" instead of destroying Koscheck. And while it's true that the UFC can't control what its fans say, it can stop playing to their baser instincts.

Nobody can effectively argue that GSP isn't a good guy. He may rub some the wrong way, or biases against people who speak another language or come from another place may blind some people's judgment, but GSP is a top athlete, an engaging person and a celebrity who has done nothing to cast any serious doubt on his integrity. Even his worst moments—saying he wasn't impressed by Matt Hughes's performance or by being allegedly greased up against BJ Penn—were minor and almost laughable. Saying you hate GSP is tantamount to saying you can't abide by honest, hard-won success. It's almost a non-issue.

GSP transcends the UFC. Dana White has admitted that GSP is a huge worldwide draw, the world's most famous Canadian athlete. "Let's fly Georges St-Pierre and Wayne Gretzky anywhere else in the world other than America and Canada [to see] who gives a shit." White told a Canadian reporter. "I like Wayne Gretzky. I was just with him, his wife and his kids a month ago over at one of the casinos here in Las Vegas. Super nice guy. Got nothing against him. Fly him over to England, fly him over to Asia, fly him to anywhere in Europe, Georges St-Pierre gets mobbed, nobody knows who the hell Wayne Gretzky is." Ever modest, GSP claims that he is not in Gretzky's class as a celebrity. He is being overly modest.

And he already is rich. Perhaps not by the standards of the top players in other professional sports, but certainly compared to the dreams of a young boy growing up in Saint Isidore. Since it was in Quebec, the payouts for *UFC 124* were not published, but with his regular fight rate, his win bonus, the $100,000 Fight of the Night bonus he shared with Koscheck, his cut of the pay-per-view money and the money from his sponsors, GSP walked out of the Bell Centre that night much richer than he came in.

And he's taking his image and his business in his own hands. On January 19, 2011, GSP issued a statement announcing that he has severed his relationship with Spencer. "They said it was amicable," a source close to the situation told *Bloody Elbow* magazine.

"Georges was just being nice. It was not. Essentially, he just fired her."

You could say that GSP has just about everything he ever wanted. He has money. He's living a comfortable life and has provided security for his family. He has fame. His legions of fans—literally millions of them around the world—will attest to that. He has respect. Shortly after the Koscheck fight, GSP was awarded Canadian Athlete of the Year from Rogers Sportsnet for the third year in a row, despite stiff competition from Sidney Crosby, who was on a tear in the NHL and had scored the Olympic-gold-medal-winning goal in overtime, and Toronto-born slugger Joey Votto, who had just won the National League MVP award. He has legions of adoring fans. On Facebook, GSP has over 1 million fans, while Crosby has about 85,000.

There's little left for GSP to prove in the welterweight class other than perhaps to hold the title the longest. He has disposed of every contender in the class. Maybe Koscheck, Alves or Fitch could mature into more well-rounded fighters, but it's unlikely they will ever be good enough to knock the still-improving champ off his block.

It's easy to predict his future. GSP will continue to fight until he feels he is no longer the best. If he loses a fight, you can bet he will rededicate himself to reclaiming the title he knows is his. It's vital to GSP to dominate the one thing more important than anything—perhaps everything—in his life since he was 12. And that's fighting. He said it best himself: "I have the best job in the world; and I want to keep doing it for a long, long time."

His next bout is scheduled for April 2011 in Toronto, another hotbed of UFC fanship, another market for the UFC to conquer, and another fight for the unstoppable GSP.

APPENDIX A:
GSP's Professional Record

In 23 professional fights, GSP has amassed a 21–2 record. Eight of his wins have come by TKO, five by submission, seven by unanimous decision and one by split decision. He has won the UFC welterweight title twice (plus one interim title) and defended it five times.

Opponent	Outcome	Fight	Date	Record/Title Status
Josh Koscheck	Win/5-round UD	UFC 124	12/11/2010	21–2/Def UFC WW Title
Dan Hardy	Win/5-round UD	UFC 111	03/27/2010	20–2/Def UFC WW Title
Thiago Alves	Win/5-round UD	UFC 100	07/11/2009	19–2/Def UFC WW Title
BJ Penn	Win/4th-round TKO (Corner)	UFC 94	01/31/2009	18–2/Def UFC WW Title
Jon Fitch	Win/5-round UD	UFC 87	08/09/2008	17–2/Def UFC WW Title
Matt Serra	Win/2nd-round TKO (Knees)	UFC 83	04/19/2008	16–2/Won UFC WW Title
Matt Hughes	Win/2nd-round Sub (Arm bar)	UFC 79	12/29/2007	15–2/Won Interim UFC WW Title

Opponent	Outcome	Fight	Date	Record/Title Status
Josh Koscheck	Win/3-round UD	UFC 74	08/25/2007	14–2
Matt Serra	Loss/1st-round TKO (Punches)	UFC 69	04/07/2007	13–2/Lost UFC WW Title
Matt Hughes	Win/2nd-round TKO (Elbows)	UFC 65	11/18/2006	13–1/Won UFC WW Title
BJ Penn	Win/3-round SD	UFC 58	03/04/2006	12–1
Sean Sherk	Win/2nd-round TKO (Strikes)	UFC 56	11/19/2005	11–1
Frank Trigg	Win/1st-round Sub (RNC)	UFC 54	08/20/2005	10–1
Jason Miller	Win/3-round UD	UFC 52	04/16/2005	9–1
Dave Strasser	Win/1st-round Sub (Kimura)	TKO 19	01/29/2005	8–1
Matt Hughes	Loss/1st-round Sub (Arm bar)	UFC 50	10/22/2004	7–1/For UFC WW Title
Jay Hieron	Win/1st-round TKO (Strikes)	UFC 48	06/19/2004	7–0
Karo Pari-syan	Win/3-round UD	UFC 46	01/31/2004	6–0/UFC debut
Pete Spratt	Win/1st-round Sub (RNC)	TKO 14	11/29/2003	5–0
Thomas Denny	Win/2nd-round TKO (Cut)	UCC 12	01/25/2003	4–0
Travis Galbraith	Win/1st-round TKO (Elbows)	UCC 11	10/11/2002	3–0/Def UCC WW Title
Justin Bruck-mann	Win/1st-round Sub (Arm bar)	UCC 10	06/15/2002	2–0/Won UCC WW Title
Ivan Men-jivar	Win/1st-round TKO (Punches)	UCC 7	01/25/2002	1–0/Professional debut

Abbreviations: TKO=technical knockout, Sub=submission, UD=unanimous decision, SD=split decision, RNC=rear-naked choke, Def=defended, WW=welterweight

APPENDIX B:
GSP's Opponents

Josh Koscheck

Nickname: Kos
Born: November 30, 1977, Waynesburg, Pennsylvania
Resides: Fresno, California
Height: 5'10"
Weight: 170 lbs.
Reach: 73.0"
Style: Wrestling, muay Thai
Record when he fought GSP: 9–1 at *UFC 74*, 15–4 at *UFC 124*
Notable: Went 42–0 in college wrestling competitions, earning Division I All-American honors four times. Has a degree in criminal justice from Edinboro University Pennsylvania.

Dan Hardy

Nickname: The Outlaw
Born: May 17, 1982, Nottingham, England

Resides: Nottingham, England
Height: 6'0"
Weight: 171 lbs.
Reach: 74.0"
Style: Taekwondo, boxing, muay Thai
Record when he fought GSP: 23–6 (one no contest)
Notable: Was in his final year of an art and design program at Nottingham Trent University when he became a professional fighter.

Thiago Alves

Nickname: Pitbull
Born: October 3, 1983, Fortaleza, Brazil
Resides: Coconut Creek, Florida
Height: 5'9"
Weight: 171 lbs.
Reach: 70"
Style: Muay Thai, Brazilian jiu-jitsu
Record when he fought GSP: 17–5
Notable: Won his first mixed martial arts fight in Brazil at age 15, moved to Florida to train full time at 19.

BJ Penn

Nickname: The Prodigy
Born: December 13, 1978, Kailua, Hawaii
Resides: Hilo, Hawaii
Height: 5'9"

Weight: 169 lbs.
Reach: 70"
Style: Brazilian jiu-jitsu, boxing
Record when he fought GSP: 10–2–1 at *UFC 58*, 13–4–1 at *UFC 94*
Notable: Is the youngest of four brothers, three of whom are named Jay Dee Penn after their father; BJ stands for his nickname, Baby Jay. Has held both welterweight and lightweight titles for the UFC. Is co-author of *Mixed Martial Arts: The Book of Knowledge* and *Why I Fight: The Belt Is Just an Accessory*.

Jon Fitch

Nickname: None
Born: February 24, 1978, Fort Wayne, Indiana
Resides: San Jose, California
Height: 6'0"
Weight: 170 lbs.
Reach: 74"
Style: Wrestling, Brazilian jiu-jitsu
Record when he fought GSP: 18–2 with one no contest
Notable: Brought a 17-fight undefeated streak into the fight with GSP. Earned a degree in physical education from Purdue University with a minor in history, and continued his education with postgraduate courses. He holds an Indiana teacher's licence.

Matt Serra

Nickname: The Terror (pronounced to rhyme with his last name)
Born: June 2, 1974, East Meadow, New York

Resides: East Meadow, New York
Height: 5'6"
Weight: 170 lbs.
Reach: 68"
Style: Brazilian jiu-jitsu, boxing
Record when he fought GSP: 9–4 at *UFC 69*, 10–4 at *UFC 83*
Notable: Won first place in Brazilian jiu-jitsu at the 1999 Pan American Games in Winnipeg. No medal was awarded as it was an exhibition sport.

Matt Hughes

Nickname: None
Born: October 13, 1973, Hillsboro, Illinois
Resides: Hillsboro, Illinois
Height: 5'9"
Weight: 170 lbs.
Reach: 73"
Style: Wrestling
Record when he fought GSP: 36–4 at *UFC 50*, 41–4 at *UFC 65*
Notable: Earned junior college All-American in wrestling in both years at Lincoln College, then was Division I All-American at Eastern Illinois University. Published his autobiography, *Made in America: The Most Dominant Champion in UFC History* with co-author Michael Malice.

Sean Sherk

Nickname: The Muscle Shark
Born: August 5, 1973, St. Francis, Minnesota

Resides: Oak Grove, Minnesota
Height: 5'6"
Weight: 155 lbs.
Reach: 67"
Style: Wrestling, Brazilian jiu-jitsu, boxing
Record when he fought GSP: 31–1–1
Notable: Former UFC lightweight champion. Unsuccessfully fought suspension after testing positive for steroids.

Frank Trigg

Nickname: Twinkle Toes
Born: May 7, 1972, Kendall, New York
Resides: Las Vegas, Nevada
Height: 5'8"
Weight: 170 lbs.
Reach: 70"
Style: Wrestling, judo
Record when he fought GSP: 12–3
Notable: Wrestled at the University of Oklahoma where he earned a degree in public affairs and administration. He also coached at Oklahoma.

Jason Miller

Nickname: Mayhem
Born: December 24, 1980, Atlanta, Georgia
Resides: Mission Viejo, California
Height: 6'1"

Weight: 185 lbs.
Reach: 77″
Style: Kickboxing, wrestling, Brazilian jiu-jitsu
Record when he fought GSP: 12–3
Notable: Has hosted both a television show and a radio show.

Dave Strasser

Nickname: None
Born: July 13, 1969, Kenosha, Wisconsin
Resides: Kenosha, Wisconsin
Height: 5′10″
Weight: 167 lbs.
Reach: 72″
Style: Boxing, Brazilian jiu-jitsu
Record when he fought GSP: 21–5–4
Notable: Has fought for 18 different mixed martial arts organizations.

Jay Hieron

Nickname: The Thoroughbred
Born: July 29, 1976, Freeport, New York
Resides: Las Vegas, Nevada
Height: 6′0″
Weight: 170 lbs.
Reach: 73″
Style: Wrestling, boxing
Record when he fought GSP: 4–0

Notable: Shortened his last name from Hieronymous because people had trouble pronouncing it correctly.

Karo Parisyan

Nickname: The Heat
Born: August 28, 1982, Yerevan, Armenia (then part of the USSR)
Resides: North Hollywood, California
Height: 5'10"
Weight: 170 lbs.
Reach: 75½"
Style: Judo
Record when he fought GSP: 10–2
Notable: Cousin Manvel Gamburyan is also a UFC fighter. Parisyan was suspended from the UFC after testing positive for banned painkillers.

Pete Spratt

Nickname: The Secret Weapon
Born: January 9, 1971, Denison, Texas
Resides: San Antonio, Texas
Height: 5'9"
Weight: 170 lbs.
Reach: 69½"
Style: Muay Thai
Record when he fought GSP: 12–6
Notable: Now teaches Brazilian jiu-jitsu.

Thomas Denny

Nickname: The Wildman
Born: April 19, Undisclosed year, Huntington Beach, California
Resides: Hesperia, California
Height: 5'10"
Weight: 170 lbs.
Reach: 70"
Style: Brazilian jiu-jitsu, wrestling, muay Thai
Record when he fought GSP: 10–9
Notable: Has fought professionally in the United States, Canada, Mexico and Japan.

Travis Galbraith

Nickname: The Gladiator
Born: 1983, Prince George, British Columbia
Resides: Edmonton, Alberta
Height: 6'0"
Weight: 185 lbs.
Reach: 72"
Style: Brazilian jiu-jitsu, wrestling, muay Thai
Record when he fought GSP: 5–1
Notable: The last Canadian fighter to take on GSP.

Justin Bruckmann

Nickname: Loaf
Born: Toronto, Ontario

Resides: Brooklin, Ontario
Height: 5'9"
Weight: 155 lbs.
Reach: 69"
Style: Judo
Record when he fought GSP: 4–1
Notable: Was UCC welterweight champion, now teaches mixed martial arts.

Ivan Menjivar

Nickname: The Pride of El Salvador
Born: May 30, 1982, El Salvador
Resides: Montreal, Quebec
Height: 5'6"
Weight: 145 lbs.
Reach: 66"
Style: Brazilian jiu-jitsu, boxing, muay Thai
Record when he fought GSP: 4–0
Notable: GSP's first professional opponent. He later became a good friend.

APPENDIX C:

GSP's training routine

- Six days a week, two sessions per day
- Each session usually lasts for an hour; the first 20 minutes are mainly warming up through stretching and the remaining 40 are "work"
- Often begins with a foam roller
- Strength training includes plyometrics and Olympic lifting, all done in rotation focusing on a specific set of muscles. He likes to do weighted chin-ups and single-leg dead lifts.
- Cardio work is mainly anaerobic, including uphill runs, sprints and sled-pulling
- Closer to a fight, he works on fight-specific exercises
- One minute of rest between drills
- Uses yoga to relax

"I always train with better wrestlers than me, better boxers than me, better jiu-jitsu guys than me. When you train with people who are better than you, it keeps challenging you. By challenging me it makes me better. It makes you better develop your skills than someone who is always training with the same people over and over again." – GSP

"When I have a fight, and the fight is getting closer, let's say a month before the fight, I don't train by just boxing, or just wrestling. I train more MMA, and what I mean by that is I make training partners come here and I mix all the training together, like kick boxing, submission, takedown on the ground, to really give me the reflex and the momentum for the fight. I do boxing, wrestling, Muay Thai, jiu-jitsu—that's the four disciplines that I do. I also do sprinting and strength conditioning." – GSP

"Georges St-Pierre's workouts are very short and they're high intensity. That's the difference between us and the majority of other people." – Firas Zahabi

"That's GSP in a nutshell: naturally gifted, trains like crazy year round, and committed to getting better. That leads to a good body every time." – Dr. John Berardi

Diet

- GSP has a personal chef in Montreal and learned about nutrition from Dr. John Berardi after the Thiago Alves fight; before that he admitted to eating lots of "crap food."

- GSP eats three whole-food meals a day with no processed sugar and no fast food. When training, he eats about 4,000 calories a day with lots of carbohydrates for use as fuel.
- He has two "super shakes" a day (made from powdered protein, berries, almond milk and fish oil) and drinks Gatorade during workouts.
- When a fight is approaching, he cuts carbs and sodium out of his diet because he believes that each gram of carbohydrate or sodium in one's body retains three grams of water. During this period, he eats only meat and vegetables and takes hot water immersion baths. He can cut 15 pounds in as little as four days this way.
- GSP generally eats a banana before a fight because it replenishes the potassium lost after a low-carb diet.

"My favorite food is tourtiere, a French Canadian dish, but unfortunately I can't eat that when I'm cutting my weight down. It's going to be for after the fight. My mother makes the best tourtiere in the world." – GSP

ACKNOWLEDGMENTS

Those who know my work know that I have written biographies and stories of interesting people who happen to be major organized crime figures. What they might not know is that my first passion when starting out as a journalist was sports, and writing a book about Georges St-Pierre has allowed me to return to those roots. As the reader has discovered in these pages, St-Pierre is a Canadian success story, emerging as a star in a sport that is rocketing to popularity. The rise of mixed martial arts and that of GSP are two stories merged into one, and it is a Canadian who is leading the phenomenon that is MMA.

To get the backstory meant watching and distilling hundreds of hours of video, listening to lots of radio appearances and reading every published interview with the man I could find. To get the present-day story, I'd like to thank the fighters, trainers and coaches, the journalists and especially the fans, who gave me their time for interviews.

On a personal note, I'd like to thank Leta Potter (or there will be hell to pay) and my family for putting up with me.

Thanks, too, to the editorial and production staff at Wiley, and the folks who market and sell my books.

Finally, I thank GSP for being such a compelling character, a good guy and a champion so worthy of having a book written about him.

INDEX